8/9/04

Robert Burns
Selected Poems and Songs

Robert Burns

Selected Poems
and Songs

Edited by
Johanna Brownell

CASTLE BOOKS

This edition published by
CASTLE BOOKS
a division of Book Sales, Inc.
114 Northfield Avenue
Edison, NJ 08837

Designed by Tony Meisel
Printed in the United States of America

ISBN 0-7858-1333-0

CONTENTS

Introduction

Robert Burns was born near the town of Ayr in Scotland on January 25, 1759. The oldest of two boys, Burns was born into a family of rural farmers. His father, William, was a hard-working man who sought to provide a good and stable life for his wife and children. But, despite his efforts, the Burns family lived in near poverty. Nevertheless, the elder Burns encouraged learning and fostered in his son a love of reading. Robert Burns finished three consecutive years of proper schooling, but it was through his own initiative that he acquired good knowledge of English, French and Latin, as well as a strong literary base in the works of giants such as Shakespeare, Pope and Homer.

By the age of 17, Robert Burns was working, along with his brother, on a farm near the town of Tarbolton. There he enrolled in a country dancing school as a way to learn social graces, as well as acquaint himself with members of the opposite sex. Burns was graced with immense charm and wit, and he easily became the object of affection for many local women for whom he, too, shared great affection. After numerous love affairs, and years of carousing the local pubs, Burns fell in love with the young Jean Armour in 1786. Jean soon became pregnant with twins. Despite his attempts to coerce her father to allow him to marry Jean, Burns could not receive the blessing of the Armour family. To make matters worse, Jean's family demanded some financial restitution for her "condition". Furthermore, Burns' relationship with Jean prompted outrage in the Presbyterian community of rural Scotland, and Burns was ultimately censured by the Kirk-session for his actions. As a result, Burns decided to emigrate to the West Indies to pursue life and career there. In order to pay for his trip, Burns published a book of his own poems, *Kilmarnock*, in 1786. The volume of poetry was met with such great success that Burns moved instead to Edinburgh where he enjoyed success as a respected man of letters. In 1787, a larger volume of Burns' poetry was published. As a result of the fame that Burns met in Edinburgh, the Armour family reconciled with Burns and he and Jean were married in 1788. In addition, Burns was able to assist his brother with his farm in Mossgiel, as well as take stock in another farm at Ellisland, where he and Jean moved for the next several years as Burns tried to settle in as a poet, farmer and family man. Sadly, Burns was not successful at Ellisland

and, in 1791, Burns moved with his family to Dumfries where he assumed a government position. But, Burns did not abandon his literary career – he succeeded in assisting with the publication of a collection of folk songs of Scotland, many of which he edited, revised or, as with "A Red, Red Rose" composed himself. Still, the pressure to support his family with a steady income drove Burns to accept a lifestyle for which he was ill-suited. In the end, the monotony of government work took its toll and, after several years of drinking and carousing, Robert Burns died of heart disease at the age of thirty eight in 1796.

Robert Burns poetry can be viewed in two parts – his English verse and his Scottish verse. Although his English poems are perfectly adequate in the history of 18th century letters, it is his Scottish poetry, primarily his songs, that characterize Burns as an important force in both the literary and socio-political history of his native land. Burns' wit, imagination and use of folk stories and themes, as well as his efforts to help collect, compose and edit over 300 folk songs of Scotland, render Burns as a keeper of the Scottish flame. Through his unique literary talents, Robert Burns gave voice and rise to Scottish folk, Scottish culture and Scottish history.

Address of Beelzebub

LONG life, my Lord, an' health be yours,
Unskaithed by hunger'd Highland boors;
Lord grant me nae duddie, desperate beggar,
Wi' dirk, claymore, and rusty trigger,
May twin auld Scotland o' a life
She likes – as butchers like a knife.

Faith you and Applecross were right
To keep the Highland hounds in sight:
I doubt na! they wad bid nae better,
Than let them ance out owre the water,
Then up among thae lakes and seas,
They'll mak what rules and laws they please:
Some daring Hancock, or a Franklin,
May set their Highland bluid a ranklin;
Some Washington again may head them,
Or some Montgomery, fearless, lead them,
Till God knows what may be effected
When by such heads and hearts directed;
Poor dunghill sons of dirt and mire
May to Patrician rights aspire!
Nae sage North now, nor sager Sackville,
To watch and premier o'er the pack vile,
An' whare will ye get Howes and Clintons
To bring them to a right repentance,
To cowe the rebel generation,
An' save the honour o' the nation?
They, an' be d—d! what right hae they
To meat, or sleep, or light o' day?
Far less-to riches, pow'r, or freedom,
But what your lordship likes to gie them?

But hear, my lord! Glengarry, hear!
Your hand's owre light to them, I fear;
Your factors, grieves, trustees, and bailies,
I canna say but they do gaylies;

They lay aside a' tender mercies,
An' tirl the hallions to the birses;
Yet while they're only poind't and herriet,
They'll keep their stubborn Highland spirit:
But smash them! crash them a' to spails,
An' rot the dyvors i' the jails!
The young dogs, swinge them to the labour!
Let wark an' hunger mak them sober!
The hizzies, if they're aughtlins fawsont,
Let them in Drury-lane be lesson'd!
An' if the wives an' dirty brats
Come thiggin at your doors an' yetts,
Flaffin wi' duds, an' grey wi' beas',
Frightin away your ducks an' geese;
Get out a horsewhip or a jowler,
The langest thong, the fiercest growler,
An' gar the tatter'd gypsies pack
Wi' a' their bastards on their back!
Go on, my Lord! I lang to meet you,
An' in my house at hame to greet you;
Wi' common lords ye shanna mingle,
The benmost neuk beside the ingle,
At my right han' assigned your seat,
'Tween Herod's hip an' Polycrate, –
Or if you on your station tarrow,
Between Almagro and Pizarro,
A seat, I'm sure ye're well deservin't;
An' till ye come – Your humble servant,
              Beelzebub.
       June 1st, Anno Mundi, 5790.

Address to the Deil

O Prince, O chief of many throned Pow'rs,
That led th' embattled seraphim to war –
             MILTON.

O THOU! whatever title suit thee,–
Auld Hornie, Satan, Nick, or Clootie!
Wha in yon cavern, grim an' sootie,
    Clos'd under hatches,
Spairges about the brunstane cootie
    To scaud poor wretches!

Hear me, auld Hangie, for a wee,
An' let poor damned bodies be;
I'm sure sma' pleasure it can gie,
    Ev'n to a deil,
To skelp an' scaud poor dogs like me,
    An' hear us squeel!

Great is thy pow'r, an' great thy fame;
Far ken'd an' noted is thy name;
An' tho' yon lowin heugh's thy hame,
    Thou travels far;
An' faith! thou's neither lag nor lame,
    Nor blate nor scaur.

Whyles, ranging like a roarin lion,
For prey a' holes an' corners tryin;
Whyles, on the strong-wing'd Tempest flyin,
    Tirlin' the kirks;
Whyles, in the human bosom pryin,
    Unseen thou lurks.

I've heard my rev'rend graunie say,
In lanely glens ye like to stray;
Or whare auld ruin'd castles gray
    Nod to the moon,
Ye fright the nightly wand'rer's way
    Wi' eldritch croon.

When twilight did my Graunie summon
To say her pray'rs, douce honest woman!
Aft yont the dyke she's heard you bummin,
    Wi' eerie drone;
Or, rustlin thro' the boortrees comin,
    Wi' heavy groan.

Ae dreary, windy, winter night,
The stars shot down wi' sklentin light,
Wi' you mysel I gat a fright,
    Ayont the lough;
Ye like a rash-buss stood in sight,
    Wi' waving sugh.

The cudgel in my nieve did shake,
Each bristl'd hair stood like a stake,
When wi' an eldritch, stoor quaick, quaick,
    Amang the springs,
Awa ye squatter'd like a drake,
    On whistling wings.

Let warlocks grim an' wither'd hags,
Tell how wi' you on ragweed nags,
They skim the muirs an' dizzy crags,
    Wi' wicked speed;
And in kirk-yards renew their leagues,
    Owre howkit dead.

Thence, countra wives wi' toil an' pain
May plunge an' plunge the kirn in vain;
For oh! the yellow treasure's taen
    By witchin skill;
An' dawtet, twal-pint Hawkie's gaen
    As yell's the Bill.

Thence, mystic knots mak great abuse,
On young guidmen, fond, keen, an' croose;
When the best wark-lume i' the house,
    By cantrip wit,
Is instant made no worth a louse,
    Just at the bit.

When thowes dissolve the snawy hoord,
An' float the jinglin icy-boord,
Then water-kelpies haunt the foord
    By your direction,
An' nighted trav'lers are allur'd
    To their destruction.

An' aft your moss-traversing Spunkies
Decoy the wight that late an drunk is:
The bleezin, curst, mischievous monkies
    Delude his eyes,
Till in some miry slough he sunk is,
    Ne'er mair to rise.

When Masons' mystic word an grip
In storms an' tempests raise you up,
Some cock or cat your rage maun stop,
    Or, strange to tell!
The youngest brither ye wad whip
    Aff straught to hell.

Lang syne, in Eden's bonie yard,
When youthfu' lovers first were pair'd,
An all the soul of love they shar'd,
    The raptur'd hour,
Sweet on the fragrant flow'ry swaird,
    In shady bow'r:

Then you, ye auld snick-drawin dog!
Ye cam to Paradise incog,
And play'd on man a cursed brogue,
    (Black be your fa'!)
An gied the infant warld a shog,
    Maist ruin'd a'.

D'ye mind that day, when in a bizz,
Wi' reeket duds an reestit gizz,
Ye did present your smoutie phiz
    'Mang better folk,
An' sklented on the man of Uzz
    Your spitefu' joke?

An' how ye gat him i' your thrall,
An' brak him out o' house and hall',
While scabs and blotches did him gall,
    Wi' bitter claw,
An' lows'd his ill-tongued, wicked scaul,
    Was warst ava?

But a' your doings to rehearse,
Your wily snares an' fechtin fierce,
Sin' that day Michael did you pierce,
    Down to this time,
Wad ding a Lallan tongue, or Erse,
    In prose or rhyme.

An' now, Auld Cloots, I ken ye're thinkin,
A certain Bardie's rantin, drinkin,
Some luckless hour will send him linkin,
    To your black pit;
But faith! he'll turn a corner jinkin,
    An' cheat you yet.

But, fare you weel, Auld Nickie-ben!
O wad ye tak a thought an' men'!
Ye aiblins might – I dinna ken –
    Still hae a stake –
I'm wae to think upo' yon den,
    Ev'n for your sake!

Address to Edinburgh

EDINA! Scotia's darling seat!
    All hail thy palaces and tow'rs,
Where once, beneath a Monarch's feet,
    Sat Legislation's sov'reign pow'rs!
From marking wildly scatt'red flow'rs,
    As on the banks of Ayr I stray'd,
And singing, lone, the lingering hours,
    I shelter in thy honour'd shade.

Here Wealth still swells the golden tide,
    As busy Trade his labours plies;
There Architecture's noble pride
    Bids elegance and splendour rise:
Here Justice, from her native skies,
    High wields her balance and her rod;
There Learning, with his eagle eyes,
    Seeks Science in her coy abode.

Thy sons, Edina, social, kind,
    With open arms the stranger hail;
Their views enlarg'd, their lib'ral mind,
    Above the narrow, rural vale:
Attentive still to sorrow's wail,
    Or modest merit's silent claim;
And never may their sources fail!
    And never envy blot their name!

Thy daughters bright thy walks adorn,
    Gay as the gilded summer sky,
Sweet as the dewy, milk-white thorn,
    Dear as the raptur'd thrill of joy!
Fair Burnet strikes th' adoring eye,
    Heaven's beauties on my fancy shine;
I see the Sire of Love on high,
    And own His work indeed divine!

There, watching high the least alarms,
	Thy rough, rude fortress gleams afar;
Like some bold veteran, grey in arms,
	And mark'd with many a seamy scar:
The pond'rous wall and massy bar,
	Grim-rising o'er the rugged rock,
Have oft withstood assailing war,
	And oft repell'd th' invader's shock.

With awe-struck thought, and pitying tears,
	I view that noble, stately dome,
Where Scotia's kings of other years,
	Fam'd heroes! had their royal home:
Alas, how chang'd the times to come!
	Their royal name low in the dust!
Their hapless race wild-wand'ring roam!
	Tho' rigid law cries out, 'twas just!

Wild beats my heart to trace your steps,
	Whose ancestors, in days of yore,
Thro' hostile ranks and ruin'd gaps
	Old Scotia's bloody lion bore:
Ev'n I who sing in rustic lore,
	Haply my sires have left their shed,
And fac'd grim danger's loudest roar,
	Bold-following where your fathers led!

Edina! Scotia's darling seat!
	All hail thy palaces and tow'rs;
Where once, beneath a Monarch's feet,
	Sat Legislation's sovereign pow'rs:
From marking wildly-scatt'red flow'rs,
	As on the banks of Ayr I stray'd,
And singing, lone, the ling'ring hours,
	I shelter in thy honour'd shade.

Address to the Toothache

WRITTEN WHEN THE AUTHOR WAS GRIEVOUSLY TORMENTED
BY THAT DISORDER.

MY curse upon your venom'd stang,
That shoots my tortur'd gums alang,
An' thro' my lugs gies mony a twang,
    Wi' gnawing vengeance,
Tearing my nerves wi' bitter pang,
    Like racking engines!

When fevers burn, or ague freezes,
Rheumatics gnaw, or colics squeezes;
Our neighbour's sympathy can ease us,
    Wi' pitying moan;
But thee-thou hell o' a' diseases,
    Aye mocks our groan.

Adown my beard the slavers trickle!
I throw the wee stools o'er the mickle,
While round the fire the giglets keckle,
    To see me loup,
While, raving mad, I wish a heckle
    Were in their doup!

O' a' the numerous human dools,
Ill hairsts, daft bargains, cutty stools, –
Or worthy frien's rak'd i' the mools,
    Sad sight to see!
The tricks o' knaves, or fash o'fools,
    Thou bear'st the gree.

Where'er that place be priests ca' hell,
Whence a' the tones o' mis'ry yell,
An' ranked plagues their numbers tell,
    In dreadfu' raw,
Thou, Toothache, surely bear'st the bell,
    Amang them a'!

O thou grim, mischief-making chiel,
That gars the notes o' discord squeel,
Till daft mankind aft dance a reel
    In gore, a shoe-thick; –
Gie a' the faes o' Scotland's weal
    A townmond's Toothache!

Ae Fond Kiss

AE fond kiss, and then we sever!
Ae fareweel, and then forever!
Deep in heart-wrung tears I'll pledge thee,
Warring sighs and groans I'll wage thee.
Who shall say that Fortune grieves him,
While the star of hope she leaves him?
Me, nae cheerfu' twinkle lights me;
Dark despair around benights me.

I'll ne'er blame my partial fancy,
Naething could resist my Nancy;
But to see her was to love her;
Love but her, and love forever.
Had we never lov'd sae kindly,
Had we never lov'd sae blindly,
Never met – or never parted,
We had ne'er been broken-hearted.

Fare thee weel, thou first and fairest!
Fare thee weel, thou best and dearest!
Thine be ilka joy and treasure,
Peace. enjoyment, love, and pleasure!
Ae fond kiss, and then we sever;
Ae fareweel, alas, forever!
Deep in heart-wrung tears I'll pledge thee,
Warring sighs and groans I'll wage thee!

Afton Water

FLOW gently, sweet Afton, among thy green braes,
Flow gently, I'll sing thee a song in thy praise;
My Mary's asleep by thy murmuring stream,
Flow gently, sweet Afton, disturb not her dream.

Thou stock-dove, whose echo resounds thro' the glen,
Ye wild whistling blackbirds in yon thorny den,
Thou green-crested lapwing, thy screaming forbear,
I charge you disturb not my slumbering fair.

How lofty, sweet Afton, thy neighbouring hills,
Far mark'd with the courses of clear winding rills;
There daily I wander as noon rises high,
My flocks and my Mary's sweet cot in my eye.

How pleasant thy banks and green valleys below,
Where wild in the woodlands the primroses blow;
There oft, as mild ev'ning sweeps over the lea,
The sweet-scented birk shades my Mary and me.

Thy crystal stream, Afton, how lovely it glides,
And winds by the cot where my Mary resides,
How wanton thy waters her snowy feet lave,
As gathering sweet flowrets she stems thy clear wave.

Flow gently, sweet Afton, among thy green braes,
Flow gently, sweet river, the theme of my lays;
My Mary's asleep by thy murmuring stream,
Flow gently, sweet Afton, disturb not her dream.

Ah, Woe Is Me, My Mother Dear

PARAPHRASE OF JEREMIAH, 15TH CHAP., 10TH VERSE.

AH, woe is me, my mother dear!
    A man of strife ye've born me:
For sair contention I maun bear;
    They hate, revile, and scorn me.

I ne'er could lend on bill or band,
    That five per cent. might blest me;
And borrowing, on the tither hand,
    The deil a ane wad trust me.

Yet I, a coin–denied wight,
    By Fortune quite discarded;
Ye see how I am, day and night,
    By lad and lass blackguarded!

Auld Lang Syne

SHOULD auld acquaintance be forgot,
And never brought to mind?
Should auld acquaintance be forgot,
And auld lang syne!

Chorus.
For auld lang syne, my dear,
For auld lang syne.
We'll tak a cup o' kindness yet,
For auld lang syne.

And surely ye'll be your pint stowp!
And surely I'll be mine!
And we'll tak a cup o'kindness yet,
For auld lang syne.
For auld, &c.

We twa hae run about the braes,
And pou'd the gowans fine;
But we've wander'd mony a weary fit,
Sin' auld lang syne.
For auld, &c.

We twa hae paidl'd in the burn,
Frae morning sun till dine;
But seas between us braid hae roar'd
Sin' auld lang syne.
For auld, &c.

And there's a hand, my trusty fere!
And gie's a hand o' thine!
And we'll tak a right gude-willie waught,
For auld lang syne.
For auld, &c.

The Author's Earnest Cry and Prayer

TO THE RIGHT HONOURABLE AND HONOURABLE SCOTCH
REPRESENTATIVES IN THE HOUSE OF COMMONS.[1]

Dearest of distillation! last and best –
– How art thou lost! –
PARODY ON MILTON

YE Irish Lords, ye Knights an' Squires,
Wha represent our brughs an' shires,
An' doucely manage our affairs
    In Parliament,
To you a simple poet's pray'rs
    Are humbly sent.

Alas! my roupet Muse is hearse!
Your Honours' hearts wi' grief 'twad pierce,
To see her sittin on her arse
    Low i' the dust,
And scriechinhout prosaic verse,
    An like to brust!

Tell them wha hae the chief direction,
Scotland an' me's in great affliction,
E'er sin' they laid that curst restriction
    On aqua-vitae;
An' rouse them up to strong conviction,
    An' move their pity.

Stand forth an' tell yon Premier youth
The honest, open, naked truth:
Tell him o' mine an' Scotland's drouth,
    His servants humble:
The muckle deevil blaw you south
    If ye dissemble!

Does ony great man glunch an' gloom?
Speak out, an' never fash your thumb!
Let posts an' pensions sink or soom
    Wi' them wha grant them;
If honestly they canna come,
    Far better want 'em.

In gath'rin votes you were na slack;
Now stand as tightly by your tack:
Ne'er claw your lug, an' fidge your back,
    An' hum an' haw;
But raise your arm, an' tell your crack
    Before them a'.

Paint Scotland greetin owre her thrissle;
Her mutchkin stowp as toom's a whissle:
An' damn'd Excisemen in a bussle,
    Seizin a Stell,
Triumphant crushin't like a mussel,
    Or limpet shell!

Then, on the tither hand present her,
A blackguard smuggler right behint her,
An' cheek-for-chow, a chuffie Vintner
    Colleaguing join,
Picking her pouch as bare as Winter
    Of a' kind coin.

Is there, that bears the name o' Scot,
But feels his heart's bluid rising hot,
To see his poor auld Mither's pot
    Thus dung in staves,
An' plunder'd o' her hindmost groat
    By gallows knaves?

Alas! I'm but a nameless wight,
Trode i' the mire out o' sight?
But could I like Montgomeries fight,
    Or gab like Boswell,[2]
There's some sark-necks I wad draw tight,
    An' tie some hose well.

God bless your Honours! can ye see't,
The kind, auld cantie Carlin greet,
An' no get warmly to your feet,
    An' gar them hear it?
An' tell them wi'a patriot-heat
    Ye winna bear it!

Some o' you nicely ken the laws,
To round the period an' pause,
An' with rhetoric clause on clause
    To mak harangues;
Then echo thro' Saint Stephen's wa's
    Auld Scotland's wrangs.

Dempster,[3] a true blue Scot I'se warran';
Thee, aith-detesting, chaste Kilkerran;[4]
An' that glib-gabbit Highland baron,
    The Laird o' Graham;[5]
An' ane, a chap that's damn'd aulfarran',
    Dundas his name:[6]

Erskine, a spunkie Norland billie;[7]
True Campbells, Frederick and Ilay;[8]
An' Livistone, the bauld Sir Willie;[9]
    An' mony ithers,
Whom auld Demosthenes or Tully
    Might own for brithers.

See sodger Hugh,[10] my watchman stented,
If poets e'er are represented;
I ken if that your sword were wanted,
    Ye'd lend a hand;
But when there's ought to say anent it,
    Ye're at a stand.

Arouse, my boys! exert your mettle,
To get auld Scotland back her kettle;
Or faith! I'll wad my new pleugh-pettle,
    Ye'll see't or lang,
She'll teach you, wi' a reekin whittle,
    Anither sang.

This while she's been in crankous mood,
Her lost Militia fir'd her bluid;
(Deil na they never mair do guid,
    Play'd her that pliskie!)
An' now she's like to rin red-wud
    About her Whisky.

An' Lord! if ance they pit her till't,
Her tartan petticoat she'll kilt,
An' durk an' pistol at her belt,
    She'll tak the streets,
An' rin her whittle to the hilt,
    I' th' first she meets!

For God sake, Sirs! then speak her fair,
An' straik her cannie wi' the hair,
An' to the *muckle house* repair,
    Wi' instant speed,
An' strive, wi' a' your wit an' lear,
    To get remead.

Yon ill tongu'd tinkler, Charlie Fox,
May taunt you wi' his jeers and mocks;
But gie him't het, my hearty cocks!
    E'en cowe the cadie!
An' send him to his dicing box
    An' sportin' lady.

Tell you guid bluid o' auld Boconnock's, [11]
I'll be his debt twa mashlum bonnocks,
An' drink his health in auld Nance Tinnock's [12]
    Nine times a-week,
If he some scheme, like tea an' winnocks,
    Was kindly seek.

Could he some commutation broach,
I'll pledge my aith in guid braid Scotch,
He needna fear their foul reproach
    Nor erudition,
Yon mixtie-maxtie, queer hotch-potch,
    The Coalition.

Auld Scotland has a raucle tongue;
She's just a devil wi' a rung;
An' if she promise auld or young
        To tak their part,
Tho' by the neck she should be strung,
        She'll no desert.

And now, ye chosen Five-and-Forty,
May still you Mither's heart support ye;
Then, tho' a minister grow dorty,
        An' kick your place,
Ye'll snap your gingers, poor an' hearty,
        Before his face.

God bless your Honours, a' your days,
Wi' sowps o' kail and brats o' claise,
In spite o' a' the thievish kaes,
        That haunt St. Jamie's!
Your humble poet sings an' prays,
        While Rab his name is.

Postscript

Let half-starv'd slaves in warmer skies
See future wines, rich-clust'ring, rise;
Their lot auld Scotland ne're envies,
        But, blythe and frisky,
She eyes her freeborn, martial boys
        Tak aff their Whisky.

What tho' their Phoebus kinder warms,
While fragrance blooms and beauty charms!
When wretches range, in famish'd swarms,
        The scented groves;
Or, hounded forth, dishonour arms
        In hungry droves!

Their gun's a burden on their shouther;
They downa bide the stink o' powther;
Their bauldest thought's a hank'ring swither

To stan' or rin,
Till skelp – a shot – they're aff, a'throwther,
   To save their skin.

But bring a Scotchman frae his hill,
Clap in his cheek a Highland gill,
Say, such is royal George's will,
      An' there's the foe!
He has nae thought but how to kill
      Twa at a blow.

Nae cauld, faint-hearted doubtings tease him;
Death comes, wi' fearless eye he sees him;
Wi' bluidy hand a welcome gies him;
      An' when he fa's,
His latest draught o' breathin lea'es him
      In faint huzzas.

Sages their solemn een may steek,
An' raise a philosophic reek,
An' physically causes seek,
      In clime an' season;
But tell me Whisky's name in Greek
      I'll tell the reason.

Scotland, my auld, respected mither!
Tho' whiles ye moistify your leather,
Till, whare ye sit on craps o' heather,
      Ye tine your dam;
Freedom an' whisky gang thegither!
      Take aff your dram!

FOOTNOTES:
1: This was written before the Act anent the Scotch distilleries, of session
1786, for which Scotland and the author return their most grateful thanks.–
R. B.
2: James Boswell of Auchinleck, the biographer of Johnson.
3: George Dempster of Dunnichen.
4: Sir Adam Ferguson of Kilkerran, Bart.
5: The Marquis of Graham, eldest son of the Duke of Montrose

6: Right Hon. Henry Dundas, M. P.

7: Probably Thomas, afterward Lord Erskine.

8: Lord Frederick Campbell, second brother of the Duke of Argyll, and Ilay Campbell, Lord Advocate for Scotland, afterward President of the Court of Session.

9: Sir Wm. Augustus Cunningham, Baronet, of Livingstone.

10: Col. Hugh Montgomery, afterward Earl of Eglinton.

11: Pitt, whose grandfather was of Boconnock in Cornwall.

12: A worthy old hostess of the author's in Mauchline, where he sometimes studies politics over a glass of gude auld Scotch Drink.-R.B.

Ballad on the American War

Tune – "Killiecrankie."

WHEN Guilford good our pilot stood
    An' did our hellim thraw, man,
Ae night, at tea, began a plea,
    Within America, man:
Then up they gat the maskin-pat,
    And in the sea did jaw, man;
An' did nae less, in full congress,
    Than quite refuse our law, man.

Then thro' the lakes Montgomery takes,
    I wat he was na slaw, man;
Down Lowrie's Burn he took a turn,
    And Carleton did ca', man:
But yet, whatreck, he, at Quebec.
    Montgomery-like did fa', man,
Wi' sword in hand, before his band,
    Amang his en'mies a', man.

Poor Tammy Gage within a cage
    Was kept at Boston-ha', man;
Till Willie Howe took o'er the knowe
    For Philadelphia, man;
Wi' sword an' gun he thought a sin
    Guid Christian bluid to draw, man;
But at New-York, wi' knife and fork,
    Sir-Loin he hacked sma', man.

Burgoygne gaed up, like spur an' whip,
    Till Fraser brave did fa', man;
Then lost his way, ae misty day,
    In Saratoga shaw, man.
Cornwallis fought as lang's he dought,
    An' did the Buckskins claw, man;
But Clinton's glaive frae rust to save,
    He hung it to the wa', man.

Then Montague, an' Guilford too,
    Began to fear a fa', man;
And Sackville dour, wha stood the stour,
    The German chief to thraw, man:
For Paddy Burke, like ony Turk,
    Nae mercy had at a', man;
An' Charlie Fox threw by the box,
    An' lows'd his tinkler jaw, man.

Then Rockingham took up the game,
    Till death did on him ca'; man;
When Shelburne meek held up his cheek,
    Conform to gospel law, man;
Saint Stephen's boys, wi' jarring noise,
    They did his measures thraw, man;
For North an' Fox united stocks,
    An' bore him to the wa', man.

Then clubs an' hearts were Charlie's cartes,
    He swept the stakes awa', man,
Till the diamond's ace, of Indian race,
    Led him a sair *faux pas,* man:
The Saxon lads, wi' loud placads,
    On Chatham's boy did ca', man;
An' Scotland drew her pipe an' blew,
    "Up, Willie, waur them a', man!"

Behind the throne then Granville's gone,
    A secret word or twa, man;
While slee Dundas arous'd the class
    Be-north the Roman wa', man:
An' Chatham's wraith, in heav'nly graith,
    (Inspired bardies saw, man),
Wi' kindling eyes, cry'd, "Willie, rise!
    Would I hae fear'd them a', man?"

But, word an' blow, North, Fox, and Co.
    Gowff'd Willie like a ba', man;
Till Suthron raise, an' coost their claise
    Behind him in a raw, man:
An' Caledon threw by the drone,
    An' did her whittle draw, man;
An' swoor fu rude, thro' dirt an' bluid,
    To mak it guid in law, man.

The Braw Wooer

Tune – "The Lothian Lassie."

LAST May, a braw wooer cam doun the lang glen,
    And sair wi' his love he did deave me;
I said, there was naething I hated like men,
    The deuce gae wi'm, to believe me, believe me,
    The deuce gae wi'm to believe me.

He spak o' the darts in my bonie black een,
    And vow'd for my love he was dying,
I said, he might die when he liked for Jean:
    The Lord forgie me for lying, for lying,
    The Lord forgie me for lying!

A weel-stocked mailen, himsel' for the laird,
    And marriage aff-hand, were his proffers;
I never loot on that I kenn'd it, or car'd;
    But thought I might hae waur offers, waur offers,
    But thought I might hae waur offers.

But what wad ye think? in a fortnight or less,
    The deil tak his taste to gae near her!
He up the lang loan to my black cousin, Bess,
    Guess ye how, the jad! I could bear her,
        could bear her,
    Guess ye how, the jad! I could bear her.

But a' the niest week, as I fretted wi' care,
    I gaed to the tryste o' Dalgarnock;
But wha but my fine fickle wooer was there,
    I glowr'd as I'd seen a warlock, a warlock,
    I glowr'd as I'd seen a warlock.

But owre my left shouther I gae him a blink,
    Lest neebors might say I was saucy;
My wooer he caper'd as he'd been in drink,
    And vow'd I was his dear lassie, dear lassie,
    And vow'd I was his dear lassie.

I spier'd for my cousin fu' couthy and sweet,
    Gin she had recover'd her hearin',
And how her new shoon fit her auld schachl't feet –
    But heavens! how he fell a swearin, a swearin,
    But heavens! how he fell a swearin.

He begged, for Gudesake, I wad be his wife,
    Or else I wad kill him wi' sorrow;
So e'en to preserve the poor body in life,
    I think I maun wed him to-morrow, to-morrow;
    I think I maun wed him to-morrow.

The Brigs Of Ayr

INSCRIBED TO JOHN BALLANTINE, ESQ., AYR.

THE simple Bard, rough at the rustic plough,
Learning his tuneful trade from ev'ry bough;
The chanting linnet, or the mellow thrush;
Hailing the setting sun, sweet, in the green thorn bush;
The soaring lark, the perching red-breast shrill,
Or deep-ton'd plovers grey, wild-whistling o'er the hill;
Shall he-nurst in the Peasant's lowly shed,
To hardy independence bravely bred,
By early poverty to hardship steel'd.
And train'd to arms in stern Misfortune's field;
Shall he be guilty of their hireling crimes,
The servile, mercenary Swiss of rhymes?
Or labour hard the panegyric close,
With all the venal soul of dedicating Prose?
No! though his artless strains he rudely sings,
And throws his hand uncouthly o'er the strings,
He glows with all the spirit of the Bard,
Fame, honest fame, his great, his dear reward.
Still, if some patron's gen'rous care he trace,
Skill'd in the secret, to bestow with grace;
When Ballantine befriends his humble name,
And hands the rustic Stranger up to fame,
With heartfelt throes his grateful bosom swells,
The godlike bliss, to give, alone excels.

      'Twas when the stacks get on their winter hap,
And thack and rape secure the toil-won crap;
Potatoe-bings are snugged up frae skaith
O' coming Winter's biting, frosty breath;
The bees, rejoicing o'er their summer toils,
Unnumber'd buds an' flow'rs' delicious spoils,
Seal'd up with frugal care in massive waxen piles,
Are doom'd by Man, that tyrant o'er the weak,
The death o' devils, smoor'd wi' brimstone reek:
The thundering guns are heard on ev'ry side,
The wounded coveys, reeling, scatter wide;

The feather'd field-mates, bound by Nature's tie,
Sires, mothers, children, in one carnage lie:
(What warm, poetic heart but inly bleeds,
And execrates man's savage, ruthless deeds!)
Nae mair the flow'r in field or meadow springs,
Nae mair the grove with airy concert rings,
Except perhaps the Robin's whistling glee,
Proud o' the height o' some bit half-lang tree:
The hoary morns precede the sunny days,
Mild, calm, serene, wide spreads the noontide blaze,
While thick the gossamour waves wanton in the rays.

'Twas in that season; when a simple Bard,
Unknown and poor-simplicity's reward,
Ae night, within the ancient brugh of Ayr,
By whim inspir'd, or haply prest wi' care,
He left his bed, and took his wayward route,
And down by Simpson's wheel'd the left about:
(Whether impell'd by all-directing Fate,
To witness what I after shall narrate;
Or whether, rapt in meditation high,
He wander'd out, he knew not where or why:)
The drowsy Dungeon-clock had number'd two,
and Wallace Tow'r had sworn the fact was true:
The tide-swoln Firth, with sullen-sounding roar,
Through the still night dash'd hoarse along the shore.
All else was hush'd as Nature's closed e'e;
The silent moon shone high o'er tower and tree;
The chilly frost, beneath the silver beam,
Crept, gently-crusting, o'er the glittering stream. –
        When, lo! on either hand the list'ning Bard,
The clanging sugh of whistling wings is heard;
Two dusky forms dart through the midnight air;
Swift as the Gos drives on the wheeling hare;
Ane on th' Auld Brig his airy shape uprears,
The other flutters o'er the rising piers:
Our warlock Rhymer instantly dexcried
The Sprites that owre the Brigs of Ayr preside.
(That Bards are second-sighted is nae joke,
And ken the lingo of the sp'ritual folk;
Fays, Spunkies, Kelpies, a', they can explain them,

And ev'n the very deils they brawly ken them).
Auld Brig appear'd of ancient Pictish race,
The very wrinkles Gothic in his face;
He seem'd as he wi' Time had warstl'd lang,
Yet, teughly doure, he bade an unco bang.
New Brig was buskit in a braw new coat,
That he, at Lon'on, frae ane Adams got;
In 's hand five taper staves as smooth 's a bead,
Wi' virls and whirlygigums at the head.
The Goth was stalking round with anxious search,
Spying the time-worn flaws in every arch;
It chanc'd his new-come neibor took his e'e,
And e'en a vexed and angry heart had he!
Wi' thieveless sneer to see his modish mien,
He, down the water, gies him this guid-e'en:-

Auld Brig

I doubt na, Frien', ye'll think ye're nae sheep-shank,
Ance ye were streekit owre frae bank to bank!
But gin ye be a brig as auld as me,
Tho' faith, that date, I doubt, ye'll never see;
There'll be, if that day come, I'll wad a boddle,
Some fewer whigmaleeries in your noddle.

New Brig

Auld Vandal! ye but show your little mense,
Just much about it wi' your scanty sense:
Will your poor, narrow foot-path of a street,
Where twa wheel-barrows tremble when they meet,
Your ruin'd, formless bulk o' stane and lime,
Compare wi' bonie Brigs o' modern time?
There's men of taste wou'd tak the Ducat-stream,
Tho' they should cast the very sark and swim,
E'er they would grate their feelings wi' the view
O' sic an ugly, Gothic hulk as you.

Auld Brig

Conceited gowk! puff'd up wi' windy pride!
This mony a year I've stood the flood an' tide;
And tho' wi' crazy eild I'm sair forfairn,
I'll be a brig when ye're a shapeless cairn!
As yet ye little ken about the matter,
But twa-three winters will inform ye better.
When heavy, dark, continued, a'-day rains,
Wi' deepening deluges o'erflow the plains;
When from the hills where springs the brawling Coil,
Or stately Lugar's mossy fountains boil;
Or where the Greenock winds his moorland course.
Or haunted Garpal draws his feeble source,
Aroused by blustering winds an' spotting thowes,
In mony a torrent down the snaw-broo rowes;
While crashing ice, borne on the rolling spate,
Sweeps dams, an' mills, an' brigs, a' to the gate;
And from Glenbuck, down to the Ratton-key,
Auld Ayr is just one lengthen'd, tumbling sea.
Then down ye'll hurl, deil nor ye never rise!
And dash the gumlie jaups up to the pouring skies!
A lesson sadly teaching, to your cost,
That Architecture's noble art is lost!

New Brig

Fine architecture, trowth, I needs must say't o't;
The Lord be thankit that we've tint the gate o't!
Gaunt, ghastly, ghaist-alluring edifices,
Hanging with threat'ning jut, like precipices;
O'er-arching, mouldy, gloom-inspiring coves,
Supporting roofs, fantastic, stony groves;
Windows and doors in nameless sculptures drest
With order, symmetry, or taste unblest;
Forms like some bedlam Statuary's dream,
The craz'd creations of misguided whim;
Forms might be worshipp'd on the bended knee,
And still the second dread command be free;
Their likeness is not found on earth, in air, or sea.
Mansions that would disgrace the building taste

Of any mason reptile, bird or beast:
Fit only for a doited monkish race,
Or frosty maids forsworn the dear embrace,
Or cuifs of later times, wha held the notion,
That sullen gloom was sterling, true devotion:
Fancies that our guid Brugh denies protection,
And soon may they expire, unblest wi' resurrection!

Auld Brig

O ye, my dear-remember'd, ancient yealings,
Were ye but here to share my wounded feelings!
Ye worthy Proveses, an' mony a Bailie,
Wha in the paths o' righteousness did toil aye;
Ye dainty Deacons, and ye douce Conveners,
To whom our moderns are but causey-cleaners!
Ye godly Councils, wha hae blest this town;
ye godly Brethren o' the sacred gown,
Wha meekly gie your hurdies to the smiters;
And (what would now be strange), ye godly Writers;
A' ye douce folk I've borne aboon the broo,
Were ye but here, what would ye say or do?
How would your spirits groan in deep vexation,
To see each melancholy alteration;
And, agonising, curse the time and place
When ye begat the base degen'rate race!
Nae langer rev'rend men, their country's glory,
In plain braid Scots hold forth a plain braid story;
Nae langer thrifty citizens, an' douce,
Meet owre a pint, or in the Council-house;
But staumrel, corky-headed, graceless Gentry,
The herryment and ruin of the country;
Men, three-parts made by tailors and by barbers,
Wha waste your weel-hain'd gear on damn'd new Brigs and
    Harbours!

New Brig

Now haud you there! for faith ye've said enough,
And muckle mair than ye can mak to through:
As for your Priesthood, I shall say but little,

Corbies and Clergy are a shot right kittle:
But, under favour o' your langer beard,
Abuse o' Magistrates might weel be spar'd;
To liken them to your auld-warld squad,
I must needs say, comparisons are odd.
In Ayr, wag-wits nae mair can hae a handle
To mouth "a Citizen," a term o' scandal:
Nae mair the Council waddles down the street,
In all the pomp of ignorant conceit;
Men wha grew wise priggin owre hops and raisins,
Or gather'd lib'ral views in bonds and seisins:
If haply Knowledge, on a random tramp,
Had shor'd them with a glimmer of his lamp,
And would to Common-sense for once betray'd them,
Plain, dull Stupidity stept kindly in to aid them.

What farther clishmaclaver aight been said,
What bloody wars, if Sprites had blood to shed,
No man can tell; but, all before their sight,
A fairy train appear'd in order bright;
Adown the glittering stream they featly danc'd;
Bright to the moon their various dresses glanc'd:
They footed o'er the wat'ry glass so neat,
The infant ice scarce bent beneath their feet:
While arts of Minstrelsy among them rung,
And soul-ennobling Bards heroic ditties sung.
O had M'Lauchlan, thairm-inspiring sage,
Been there to hear this heavenly band engage,
When thro' his dear strathspeys they bore with Highland rage;
Or when they struck old Scotia's melting airs,
The lover's raptured joys or bleeding cares;
How would his Highland lug been nobler fir'd,
And ev'n his matchless hand with finer touch inspir'd!
No guess could tell what instrument appear'd,
But all the soul of Music's self was heard;
Harmonious concert rung in every part,
While simple melody pour'd moving on the heart.
    The Genius of the Stream in front appears,
A venerable Chief, advanc'd in years;
His hoary head with water-lilies crown'd,
His manly leg with garter-tangle bound.

Next came the loveliest pair in all the ring,
Sweet female Beauty hand in hand with Spring;
Then, crown'd with flow'ry hay, came Rural Joy,
And Summer, with his fervid-beaming eye;
All-cheering Plenty, with her flowing horn,
Led yellow Autumn wreath'd with nodding corn;
Then Winter's time-bleach'd locks did hoary show,
By Hospitality with cloudless brow:
Next followed Courage with his martial stride,
From where the Feal wild-woody coverts hide;
Benevolence, with mild, benignant air,
A female form, came from the tow'rs of Stair;
Learning and Worth in equal measures trode,
From simple Catrine, their long-lov'd abode:
Last, white-rob'd Peace, crown'd with a hazel wreath,
To rustic Agriculture did bequeath
The broken, iron instruments of death:
At sight of whom our Sprites forgat their kindling wrath.

Come, Let Me Take Thee To My Breast

Tune – "Cauld Kail".

COME, let me take thee to my breast,
    And pledge we ne'er shall sunder;
And I shall spurn as vilest dust
    The world's wealth and grandeur:
And do I hear my Jeanie own
    That equal transports move her?
I ask for dearest life alone,
    That I may live to love her.

Thus, in my arms, wi' all thy charms,
    I clasp my countless treasure;
I'll seek nae mair o' heaven to share,
    Tha sic a moment's pleasure:
And by thy een sae bonie blue,
    I swear I'm thine for ever!
And on thy lips I seal my vow,
    And break it shall I never.

The Cotter's Saturday Night

INSCRIBED TO ROBERT AIKEN, ESQ., OF AYR.

Let not Ambition mock their useful toil,
Their homely joys and destiny obscure;
Nor Grandeur hear with a disdainful smile,
The short and simple annals of the Poor.
GRAY.

MY lov'd, my honour'd, much respected friend!
   No mercenary bard his homage pays;
With honest pride, I scorn each selfish end:
   My dearest meed a friend's esteem and praise:
To you I sing, in simple Scottish lays,
   The lowly train in life's sequester'd scene;
The native feelings strong, the guileless ways;
   What Aiken in a cottage would have been;
Ah! tho' his worth unknown, far happier there, I ween.

November chill blaws loud wi' angry sugh;
   The short'ning winter day is near a close;
The miry beasts retreating frae the pleugh;
   The black'ning trains o' craws to their repose:
The toil-worn Cotter frae his labour goes,
   This night his weekly moil is at an end,
Collects his spades, his mattocks and his hoes,
   Hoping the morn in ease and rest to spend,
And weary, o'er the moor, his course does hameward
bend.

At length his lonely cot appears in view,
   Beneath the shelter of an aged tree;
Th' expectant wee-things, toddlin, stacher through
   To meet their Dad, wi' flichterin noise an' glee.
His wee bit ingle, blinkin bonilie,
   His clean hearth-stane, his thrifty wifie's smile,
The lisping infant prattling on his knee,
   Does a' his weary carking cares beguile,
An' makes him quite forget his labour an' his toil.

Belyve, the elder bairns come drapping in,
    At service out, amang the farmers roun';
Some ca' the pleugh, some herd, some tentie rin
    A cannie errand to a neibor town:
Their eldest hope, their Jenny, woman-grown,
    In youthfu' bloom, love sparkling in her e'e,
Comes hame, perhaps, to shew a braw new gown,
    Or deposite her sair-won penny-fee,
To help her parents dear, if they in hardship be.

With joy unfeign'd, brothers and sisters meet,
    An' each for other's weelfare kindly spiers:
The social hours, swift-wing'd, unnotic'd fleet;
    Each tells the uncos that he sees or hears;
The parents partial eye their hopeful years;
    Anticipation forward points the view.
The mother, wi' her needle an' her sheers,
    Gars auld claes look amaist as weel's the new;
The father mixes a' wi' admonition due.

Their master's an' their mistress's command
    The younkers a' are warned to obey;
An' mind their labours wi' an eydent hand,
    An' ne'er tho' out o' sight, to jauk or play:
An' O! be sure to fear the Lord alway,
    "An' mind your duty, duly, morn an' night!
Lest in temptation's path ye gang astray,
    Implore His counsel and assisting might:
They never sought in vain that sought the Lord aright!"

But hark! a rap comes gently to the door.
    Jenny, wha kens the meaning o' the same,
Tells how a neebor lad cam o'er the moor,
    To do some errands, and convoy her hame.
The wily mother sees the conscious flame
    Sparkle in Jenny's e'e, and flush her cheek;
Wi' heart-struck, anxious care, inquires his name,
    While Jenny hafflins is afraid to speak;
Weel-pleas'd the mother hears, it's nae wild, worthless rake.

Wi' kindly welcome Jenny brings him ben;
      A strappan youth; he takes the mother's eye;
Blythe Jenny sees the visit's no ill ta'en;
      The father cracks of horses, pleughs, and kye.
The youngster's artless heart o'erflows wi' joy,
      But, blate and laithfu', scarce can weel behave;
The mother, wi' a woman's wiles, can spy
      What maks the youth sae bashfu' an' sae grave;
Weel pleas'd to think her bairn's respected like the lave.

O happy love! where love like this is found!
      O heart-felt raptures! bliss beyond compare!
I've paced much this weary, mortal round,
      And sage experience bids me this declare –
"If Heaven a draught of heavenly pleasure spare,
      One cordial in this melancholy vale,
'Tis when a youthful, loving, modest pair,
      In other's arms breathe out the tender tale,
Beneath the milk-white thorn that scents the ev'ning gale.

Is there, in human form, that bears a heart,
      A wretch! a villain! lost to love and truth!
That can with studied, sly, ensnaring art
      Betray sweet Jenny's unsuspecting youth?
Curse on his perjur'd arts! dissembling smooth!
      Are honour, virtue, conscience, all exil'd?
Is there no pity, no relenting ruth,
      Points to the parents fondling o'er their child,
Then paints the ruin'd maid, and their distraction wild?

But now the supper crowns their simple board,
      The halesome parritch, chief of Scotia's food;
The soupe their only hawkie does afford,
      That 'yont the hallan snugly chows her cood.
The dame brings forth, in complimental mood,
      To grace the lad, her weel-hain'd kebbuck, fell.
An' aft he's prest, an' aft he ca's it guid;
      The frugal wifie, garrulous, will tell,
How 'twas a towmond auld, sin' lint was i' the bell.

The cheerfu' supper done, wi' serious face,
　　They round the ingle form a circle wide;
The sire turns o'er, with patriarchal grace,
　　The big ha'-Bible, ance his father's pride:
His bonnet rev'rently is laid aside,
　　His lyart haffets wearing thin and bare;
Those strains that once did sweet in Zion glide,
　　He wales a portion with judicious care;
And, "Let us worship God," he says with solemn air.

They chant their artless notes in simple guise;
　　They tune their hearts, by far the noblest aim:
Perhaps Dundee's wild-warbling measures rise,
　　Or plaintive Martyrs, worthy of the name;
Or noble Elgin beets the heaven-ward flame,
　　The sweetest far of Scotia's holy lays.
Compar'd with these, Italian trills are tame;
　　The tickl'd ear no heart-felt raptures raise;
Nae unison hae they, with our Creator's praise.

The priest-like father reads the sacred page,
　　How Abram was the friend of God on high;
Or Moses bade eternal warfare wage
　　With Amalek's ungracious progeny;
Or how the royal bard did groaning lie
　　Beneath the stroke of Heaven's avenging ire;
Or Job's pathetic plaint, and wailing cry;
　　Or rapt Isaiah's wild, seraphic fire;
Or other holy seers that tune the sacred lyre.

Perhaps the Christian volume is the theme,
　　How guiltless blood for guilty man was shed;
How He, who bore in Heaven the second name
　　Had not on earth whereon to lay His head:
How His first followers and servants sped;
　　The precepts sage they wrote to many a land:
How he, who lone in Patmos banished,
　　Saw in the sun a mighty angel stand,
And heard great Bab'lon's doom pronounc'd by Heaven's
　　command.

Then kneeling down to Heaven's Eternal King,
    The saint, the father, and the husband prays:
Hope "springs exulting on triumphant wing,"
    That thus they all shall meet in future days:
There ever bask in uncreated rays,
    No more to sigh or shed the bitter tear,
Together hymning their Creator's praise,
    In such society, yet still more dear,
While circling Time moves round in an eternal sphere.

Compar'd with this, how poor Religion's pride
    In all the pomp of method and of art,
When men display to congregations wide
    Devotion's ev'ry grace except the heart!
The Power, incens'd, the pageant will desert,
    The pompous strain, the sacerdotal stole;
But haply in some cottage far apart
    May hear, well pleas'd, the language of the soul;
And in his Book of Life the inmates poor enrol.

Then homeward all take off their sev'ral way;
    The youngling cottagers retire to rest;
The parent-pair their secret homage pay,
    And proffer up to Heav'n the warm request,
That He who stills the raven's clam'rous nest,
    And decks the lily fair in flow'ry pride,
Would, in the way His wisdom sees the best,
    For them and for their little ones provide;
But chiefly, in their hearts with grace divine preside.

From scenes like these old Scotia's grandeur springs,
    That makes her lov'd at home, rever'd abroad:
Princes and lords are but the breath of kings,
    "An honest man's the noblest work of God":
And certes, in fair Virtue's heavenly road,
    The cottage leaves the palace far behind:
What is a lordling's pomp? a cumbrous load,
    Disguising oft the wretch of human kind,
Studied in arts of hell, in wickedness refin'd!

O Scotia! my dear, my native soil!
    For whom my warmest wish to Heaven is sent!
Long may thy hardy sons of rustic toil
    Be blest with health, and peace, and sweet content!
And, oh! may Heaven their simple lives prevent
    From luxury's contagion, weak and vile!
Then, howe'er crowns and coronets be rent,
    A virtuous populace may rise the while,
And stand a wall of fire around their much-lov'd isle.

O Thou! who pour'd the patriotic tide
    That stream'd thro' Wallace's undaunted heart,
Who dar'd to nobly stem tyrannic pride,
    Or nobly die, the second glorious part,–
(The patriot's God peculiarly thou art,
    His friend, inspirer, guardian, and reward!)
O never, never Scotia's realm desert,
    But still the patriot, and the patriot-bard,
In bright succession raise, her ornament and guard!

The Death and Dying Words
of Poor Mailie, The Author's Only Pet Yowe

AN UNCO MOURNFUL TALE

AS Mailie, an' her lambs thegither,
Was ae day nibbling on the tether,
Upon her cloot she coost a hitch,
An' owre she warsl'd in the ditch:
There, groaning, dying, she did lie,
When Hughoc he cam doytin by.

Wi' glowrin een, and lifted han's
Poor Hughoc like a statue stan's;
He saw her days were near-hand ended,
But, waels my heart! he could na mend it!
He gaped wide, but naething spak,
At langth poor Mailie silence brak.

O thou, whase lamentable face
Appears to mourn my woefu' case!
My dying words attentive hear,
An' bear them to my Master dear.

"Tell him, if e'er again he keep
As muckle gear as buy a sheep,
O, bid him never tie them mair,
Wi' wicked strings o' hemp or hair!
But ca' them out to park or hill,
An' let them wander at their will:
So may his flock increase, an' grow
To scores o' lambs, an' packs o' woo'!

"Tell him, he was a Master kin',
An' aye was guid to me an' mine;
An, now my dying charge I gie him,
My helpless lambs, I trust them wi' him.

"O, bid him save their harmless lives,
Frae dogs, an' tods, an' butcher's knives!

But gie them guid cow-milk their fill,
Till they be fit to fend themsel:
An' tent them duly, e'en an' morn,
Wi' taets o' hay an' ripps o' corn.

"An' may they never learn the gaets,
Of ither vile, wanrestfu' pets!
To slink thro' slaps, an' reave an' steal
At stacks o' pease or stocks o' kail!
So may they, like their great Forbears,
For mony a year come thro' the sheers:
So wives will gie them bits o' bread,
An' bairns greet for them when they're dead.

"My poor toop-lamb, my son an' heir,
O, bid law breed him up wi' care!
An' if he live to be a beast,
To pit some havins in his breast!
An' warn him, what I winna name,
To stay content, wi' yowes at hame;
An' no to rin and' waer his cloots,
Like other menseless, graceless brutes.

"An' neist, my yowie, silly thing,
Gude keep thee frae a tether string!
O, may thou ne'er forgather up
Wi' ony blastit, moorland toop;
But aye keep mind to moop an' mell,
Wi' sheep o' credit like thysel!

"And now, my bairns, wi' my last breath,
I lea'e my blessin wi' you baith:
An' when you think upo' your Mither,
Mind to be kind to ane anither.
"Now, honest Hughoc, dinna fail,
To tell my master a' my tale;
An' bid him bum this cursed tether,
An' for thy pains thou'se get my blather."

This said, poor Mailie turn'd her head,
And clos'd her een amang the dead!

Despondency: An Ode

OPPRESS'D with grief, oppress'd with care,
A burden more than I can bear,
   I set me down and sigh:
O life! thou art a galling load,
Along a rough, a weary road,
   To wretches such as I!
Dim backward as I cast my view,
   What sick'ning scenes appear!
What sorrows yet may pierce me through,
   Too justly I may fear!
     Still caring, despairing,
       Must be my bitter doom;
     My woes here shall close ne'er
       But with the closing tomb!

Happy! ye sons of busy life,
Who, equal to the bustling strife,
   No other view regard!
Ev'n when the wished end's deny'd,
Yet while the busy means are ply'd,
   They bring their own reward:
Whilst I, a hope-abandon'd wight,
   Unfitted with an aim,
Meet ev'ry sad returning night,
   And joyless morn the same!
     You, bustling, and justling,
       Forget each grief and pain;
     I, listless, yet restless,
       Find ev'ry prospect vain.

How blest the Solitary's lot,
Who, all-forgetting, all forgot,
   Within his humble cell,
The cavern, wild with tangling roots,
Sits o'er his newly gather'd fruits,
   Beside his crystal well!
Or haply, to his ev'ning thought,
   By unfrequented stream,

The ways of men are distant brought,
 A faint-collected dream;
  While praising, and raising
   His thoughts to heav'n on high,
  As wand'ring, meand'ring,
   He views the solemn sky.

Than I, no lonely hermit plac'd
Where never human footstep trac'd,
 Less fit to play the part,
The lucky moment to improve,
And just to stop, and just to move,
 With self-respecting art:
But ah! those pleasures, loves, and joys,
 Which I too keenly taste,
The Solitary can despise,
  Can want, and yet be blest!
   He needs not, he heeds not,
    Or human love or hate;
   Whilst I here must cry here
    At perfidy ingrate!

O, enviable, early days,
When dancing thoughtless pleasure's maze,
 To care, to guilt unknown!
How ill exchang'd for riper times,
To feel the follies, or the crimes,
 Of others, or my own!
Ye tiny elves that guiltless sport,
 Like linnets in the bush,
Ye little know the ills ye court,
  When manhood is your wish!
   The losses, the crosses,
    That active man engage;
   The fears all, the tears all,
    Of dim-declining age!

Epistle To A Young Friend

I LANG hae thought, my youthfu' friend,
    A something to have sent you,
Tho' it should serve nae ither end
    Than just a kind memento,
But how the subject-theme may gang,
    Let time and chance determine;
Perhaps, it may turn out a sang:
    Perhaps, turn out a sermon.

Ye'll try the world soon, my lad;
    And, Andrew dear, believe me,
Ye'll find mankind an unco squad,
    And muckle they may grieve ye:
For care and trouble set your thought,
    Ev'n when your end's attained;
And a' your views may come to nought,
    Where ev'ry nerve is strained.

I'll no say, men are villains a';
    The real, harden'd wicked,
Wha hae nae check but human law,
    Are to a few restricked;
But, Och! mankind are unco weak,
    An' little to be trusted;
If self the wavering balance shake,
    It's rarely right adjusted!

Yet they wha fa' in fortune's strife,
    Their fate we should na censure;
For still, th' important end of life
    They equally may answer;
A man may hae an honest heart,
    Tho' poortith hourly stare him;
A man may tak a neibor's part,
    Yet hae nae cash to spare him.

Aye free, aff han', your story tell,
    When wi' a bosom crony;
But still keep something to yoursel,
    Ye scarcely tell to ony,
Conceal yoursel' as weel's ye can
    Frae critical dissection;
But keek thro' ev'ry other man,
    Wi' sharpen'd, sly inspection.

The sacred lowe o' weel-plac'd love,
    Luxuriantly indulge it;
But never tempt th' illicit rove,
    Tho' naething should divulge it:
I waive the quantum o' the sin,
    The hazard o' concealing;
But, Och! it hardens a' within,
    And petrifies the feeling!

To catch dame Fortune's golden smile,
    Assiduous wait upon her;
And gather gear by ev'ry wile
    That's justified by honour;
Not for to hide it in a hedge,
    Nor for a train attendant;
But for the glorious privilege
    Of being independent.

The fear o' hell's a hangman's whip,
    To haud the wretch in order;
But where ye feel your honour grip,
    Let that aye be your border;
Its slightest touches, instant pause –
    Debar a' side pretences;
And resolutely keep its laws,
    Uncaring consequences.

The great Creator to revere,
　　Must sure become the creature;
But still the preaching cant forbear,
　　And ev'n the rigid feature:
Yet ne'er with wits profane to range,
　　Be complaisance extended;
An Atheist-laugh's a poor exchange
　　For Deity offended!

When ranting round in pleasure's ring,
　　Religion may be blinded;
Or if she gie a random sting,
　　It may be little minded;
But when on life we're tempest driv'n,
　　A conscience but a canker –
A correspondence fix'd wi' Heaven,
　　Is sure a noble anchor!

Adieu, dear, amiable Youth!
　　Your heart can ne'er be wanting!
May prudence, fortitude, and truth,
　　Erect your brow undaunting!
In ploughman phrase, "God send you speed,"
　　Still daily to grow wiser;
And may ye better reck the rede,
　　Then ever did th' Adviser!

Epitaph On My Father

O YE, whose cheek the tear of pity stains,
    Draw near with pious rev'rence, and attend!
Here lie the loving husband's dear remains,
    The tender father, and the gen'rous friend;

The pitying heart that felt for human woe,
    The dauntless heart that fear'd no human pride;
The friend of man, to vice alone a foe;
    "For ev'n his failings lean'd to virtue's side."

The First Six Verses of the Nineteenth Psalm Versified

O THOU, the first, the greatest friend
 Of all the human race!
Whose strong right hand has ever been
 Their stay and dwelling place!

Before the mountains heav'd their heads
 Beneath Thy forming hand,
Before this ponderous globe itself
 Arose at Thy command;

That Pow'r which rais'd and still upholds
 This universal frame,
From countless, unbeginning time
 Was ever still the same.

Those mighty periods of years
 Which seem to us so vast,
Appear no more before Thy sight
 Than yesterday that's past.

Thou giv'st the word:, Thy creature, man,
 Is to existence brought;
Again Thou say'st, "Ye sons of men,
 Return ye into nought!"

Thou layest them, with all their cares,
 In everlasting sleep;
As with it flow Thou tak'st them off
 With overwhelming sweep.

They flourish like the morning flow'r,
 In beauty's pride array'd;
But long ere night cut down it lies
 All wither'd and decay'd.

For A' That and A' That

IS there, for honest poverty,
    That hings his head, and a' that?
The coward slave, we pass him by,
    We dare be poor for a' that!
        For a' that, and a' that,
            Our toils obscure, and a' that;
        The rank is but the guinea's stamp;
            The man's the gowd for a' that,

What tho' on hamely fare we dine,
    Wear hoddin-gray, an' a' that;
Gie fools their silks, and knaves their wine,
    A man's a man for a' that.
        For a' that, and a' that,
            Their tinsel show and a' that;
        The honest man, tho' e'er sae poor,
            Is King o' men for a' that.

Ye see yon birkie, ca'd a lord
    Wha struts, an' stares, and a' that;
Tho' hundreds worship at his word,
    He's but a coof for a' that:
        For a' that, and a' that,
            His riband, star, and a' that,
        The man o' independent mind,
            He looks and laughs at a' that.

A prince can mak a belted knight,
    A marquis, duke, and a' that;
But an honest man's aboon his might,
    Guid faith he mauna fa' that!
        For a' that, and a' that,
            Their dignities, and a' that,
        The pith o' sense, an' pride o' worth,
            Are higher rank than a' that.

Then let us pray that come it may,
　　As come it will for a' that,
That sense and worth, o'er a' the earth,
　　May bear the gree, an' a' that.
　　　　For a' that, and a' that,
　　　　　　It's coming yet, for a' that,
　　That man to man, the warld o'er,
　　　　　　Shall brothers be for a' that.

Frae the Friends and Land I Love

Tune – "Carron Side."

FRAE the friends and land I love,
    Driv'n by Fortune's felly spite;
Frae my best belov'd I rove,
    Never mair to taste delight:
Never mair maun hope to find
    Ease frae toil, relief frae care;
When Remembrance wracks the mind,
    Pleasures but unveil despair.

Brightest climes shall mirk appear,
    Desert ilka blooming shore,
Till the Fates, nae mair severe,
    Friendship, love, and peace restore,
Till Revenge, wi' laurel'd head,
    Bring our banished hame again;
And ilk loyal, bonie lad
    Cross the seas, and win his ain.

Fragment – Her Flowing Locks

HER flowing locks, the raven's wing,
    Adown her neck and bosom hing;
How sweet unto that breast to cling,
    And round that neck entwine her!

Her lips are roses wat wi' dew!
    O, what a feast her bonie mou'!
Her cheeks a mair celestial hue,
    A crimson still diviner!

Fragment – The Mauchline Lady

Tune – "I had a horse, I had nae mair."

WHEN first I came to Stewart Kyle,
My mind it was na steady,
Where'er I gaed, where'er I rade,
A mistress still I had aye:

But when I came roun' by Mauchline town,
Not dreadin onie body,
My heart was caught, before I thought,
And by a Mauchline lady.

Halloween [1]

The following poem will, by many readers, be well enough understood; but for the sake of those who are unacquainted with the manners and traditions of the country where the scene is cast, notes are added to give some account of the principal charms and spells of that night, so big with prophecy to the peasantry in the west of Scotland. The passion of prying into futurity makes a striking part of the history of human nature in its rude state, in all ages and nations; and it may be some entertainment to a philosophic mind, if any such honour the author with a perusal, to see the remains of it among the more unenlightened in our own. – R.B.

> *Yes! let the rich deride, the proud disdain,*
> *The simple pleasure of the lowly train;*
> *To me more dear, congenial to my heart,*
> *One native charm, than all the gloss of art.*
> GOLDSMITH.

UPON that night, when fairies light
    On Cassilis Downans[2] dance,
Or owre the lays, in splendid blaze,
    On sprightly coursers prance;
Or for Colean the rout is ta'en,
    Beneath the moon's pale beams;
There, up the Cove[3], to stray an' rove,
    Amang the rocks and streams
        To sport that night:

Amang the bonie winding banks,
    Where Doon rins, wimplin, clear;
Where Bruce[4] ance rul'd the martial ranks,
    An' shook his Carrick spear;
Some merry, friendly, countra-folks
    Together did convene,
To burn their nits, an' pou their stocks,
    An' haud their Halloween
        Fu' blythe that night.

The lasses feat, an' cleanly neat,
    Mair braw than when they're fine;
Their faces blythe, fu' sweetly kythe,
    Hearts leal, an' warm, an' kin':
The lads sae trig, wi' wooer-babs
    Weel-knotted on their garten;
Some unco blate, an' some wi' gabs
    Gar lasses' hearts gang startin
        Whiles fast at night.

Then, first an' foremost, thro' the kail,
    Their stocks[5] maun a' be sought ance;
They steek their een, and grape an' wale
    For muckle anes, an' straught anes.
Poor hav'rel Will fell aff the drift,
    An' wandered thro' the "bow-kail,"
An' pou't for want o' better shift
    A runt was like a sow-tail
        Sae bow't that night.

Then, straught or crooked, yird or nane,
    They roar an' cry a' throu'ther;
The vera wee-things, toddlin, rin,
    Wi' stocks out owre their shouther:
An' gif the custock's sweet or sour,
    Wi' joctelegs they taste them;
Syne coziely, aboon the door,
    Wi' cannie care, they've plac'd them
        To lie that night.

The lassies staw frae 'mang them a',
    To pou their stalks o' corn;[6]
But Rab slips out, an' jinks about,
    Behint the muckle thorn:
He grippit Nelly hard and fast:
    Loud skirl'd a' the lasses;
But her tap-pickle maist was lost,
    Whan kiutlin in the fause-house[7]
        Wi' him that night.

The auld guid-wife's weel-hoordit nits[8]
    Are round an' round divided,
An' mony lads an' lasses' fates
    Are there that night decided:
Some kindle couthie side by side,
    And burn thegither trimly;
Some start awa wi' saucy pride,
    An' jump out owre the chimlie
        Fu' high that night.

Jean slips in twa, wi' tentie e'e;
    Wha 'twas, she wadna tell;
But this is *Jock*, an' this is *me*,
    She says in to hersel':
He bleez'd owre her, an' she owre him,
    As they wad never mair part:
Till fuff! he started up the lum,
    An' Jean had e'en a sair heart
        To see't that night.

Poor Willie, wi' his bow-kail runt,
    Was brunt wi' primsie Mallie;
An' Mary, nae doubt, took the drunt,
    To be compar'd to Willie:
Mall's nit lap out, wi' pridefu' fling,
    An' her ain fit, it brunt it;
While Willie lap, and swore by jing,
    'Twas just the way he wanted
        To be that night.

Nell had the fause-house in her min',
    She pits hersel an' Rob in;
In loving bleeze they sweetly join,
    Till white in ase they're sobbin:
Nell's heart was dancin at the view;
    She whisper'd Rob to leuk for't:
Rob, stownlins, prie'd her bonie mou',
    Fu' cozie in the neuk for't,
        Unseen that night.

But Merran sat behint their backs,
    Her thoughts on Andrew Bell;
She lea'es them gashin at their cracks,
    An' slips out-by hersel';
She thro' the yard the nearest taks,
    An' for the kiln she goes then,
An' darklins grapit for the bauks,
    And in the blue-clue[9] throws then,
        Right fear't that night.

An' ay she win't, an' ay she swat –
    I wat she made nae jaukin;
Till something held within the pat,
    Good Lord! but she was quaukin!
But whether 'twas the deil himsel,
    Or whether 'twas a bauk-en',
Or whether it was Andrew Bell,
    She did na wait on talkin
        To spier that night.

Wee Jenny to her graunie says,
    "Will ye go wi' me, graunie?
I'll eat the apple at the glass,[10]
    I gat frae uncle Johnie:"
She fuff't her pipe wi' sic a lunt,
    In wrath she was sae vap'rin,
She notic't na an aizle brunt
    Her braw, new, worset apron
        Out thro' that night.

"Ye little skelpie-limmer's face!
    I daur you try sic sportin,
As seek the foul thief ony place,
    For him to spae your fortune:
Nae doubt but ye may get a sight!
    Great cause ye hae to fear it;
For mony a ane has gotten a fright,
    An' liv'd an' died deleerit,
        On sic a night.

"Ae hairst afore the Sherra-moor,
    I mind't as weel's yestreen –
I was a gilpey then, I'm sure
    I was na past fyfteen:
The simmer had been cauld an' wat,
    An' stuff was unco green;
An' eye a rantin kirn we gat,
    An' just on Halloween
        It fell that night.

"Our stibble-rig was Rab M'Graen,
    A clever, sturdy fallow;
His sin gat Eppie Sim wi' wean,
    That lived in Achmacalla:
He gat hemp-seed,[11] I mind it weel,
    An'he made unco light o't;
But mony a day was by himsel',
    He was sae sairly frighted
        That vera night."

Then up gat fechtin Jamie Fleck,
    An' he swoor by his conscience,
That he could saw hemp-seed a peck;
    For it was a' but nonsense:
The auld guidman raught down the pock,
    An' out a handfu' gied him;
Syne bad him slip frae' mang the folk,
    Sometime when nae ane see'd him,
        An' try't that night.

He marches thro' amang the stacks,
    Tho' he was something sturtin;
The graip he for a harrow taks,
    An' haurls at his curpin:
And ev'ry now an' then, he says,
    "Hemp-seed I saw thee,
An' her that is to be my lass
    Come after me, an' draw thee
        As fast this night."

He wistl'd up "Lord Lennox" March
    To keep his courage cheery;
Altho' his hair began to arch,
    He was sae fley'd an' eerie:
Till presently he hears a squeak,
    An' then a grane an' gruntle;
He by his shouther gae a keek,
    An' tumbled wi' a wintle
        Out-owre that night.

He roar'd a horrid murder-shout,
    In dreadfu' desperation!
An' young an' auld come rinnin out,
    An' hear the sad narration:
He swoor 'twas hilchin Jean M'Craw,
    Or crouchie Merran Humphie –
Till stop! she trotted thro' them a';
    And wha was it but grumphie
        Asteer that night?

Meg fain wad to the barn gaen,
    To winn three wechts o' naething;[12]
But for to meet the deil her lane,
    She pat but little faith in:
She gies the herd a pickle nits,
    An' twa red cheekit apples,
To watch, while for the barn she sets,
    In hopes to see Tam Kipples
        That vera night.

She turns the key wi' cannie thraw,
    An' owre the threshold ventures;
But first on Sawnie gies a ca',
    Syne baudly in she enters:
A ratton rattl'd up the wa',
    An' she cry'd Lord preserve her!
An' ran thro' midden-hole an' a',
    An' pray'd wi' zeal and fervour,
        Fu' fast that night.

They hoy't out Will, wi' sair advice;
    They hecht him some fine braw ane;
It chanc'd the stack he faddom't thrice[13]
    Was timmer-propt for thrawin:
He taks a swirlie auld moss-oak
    For some black, grousome carlin;
An' loot a winze, an' drew a stroke,
    Till skin in blypes cam haurlin
        Aff's nieves that night.

A wanton widow Leezie was,
    As cantie as a kittlen;
But och! that night, amang the shaws,
    She gat a fearfu' settlin!
She thro' the whins, an' by the cairn,
    An' owre the hill gaed scrievin;
Whare three lairds' lan's met at a burn,[14]
    To dip her left sark-sleeve in,
        Was bent that night.

Whiles owre a linn the burnie plays,
    As thro' the glen it wimpl't;
Whiles round a rocky scar it strays,
    Whiles in a wiel it dimpl't;
Whiles glitter'd to the nightly rays,
    Wi' bickerin', dancin' dazzle;
Whiles cookit undeneath the braes,
    Below the spreading hazel
        Unseen that night.

Amang the brachens, on the brae,
    Between her an' the moon,
The deil, or else an outler quey,
    Gat up an' ga'e a croon:
Poor Leezie's heart maist lap the hool;
    Near lav'rock-height she jumpit,
But mist a fit, an' in the pool
    Out-owre the lugs she plumpit,
        Wi' a plunge that night.

In order, on the clean hearth-stane,
 The luggies[15] three are ranged;
An' ev'ry time great care is ta'en
 To see them duly changed:
Auld uncle John, wha wedlock's joys
 Sin' Mar's-year did desire,
Because he gat the toom dish thrice,
 He heav'd them on the fire
  In wrath that night.

Wi' merry sangs, an' friendly cracks,
 I wat they did na weary;
And unco tales, an' funnie jokes –
 Their sports were cheap an' cheery:
Till butter'd sowens,[16] wi' fragrant lunt,
 Set a' their gabs a-steerin;
Syne, wi' a social glass o' strunt,
 They parted aff careerin
  Fu' blythe that night.

FOOTNOTES:

1: Is thought to be a night when witches, devils, and other mischief making beings are abroad on their baneful midnight errands; particularly those
aerial people, the fairies, are said on that night to hold a grand anniver-
sary,.-R.B.

2: Certain little, romantic, rocky, green hills, in the neighbourhood of the
ancient seat of the Earls of Cassilis.-R.B.

3: A noted cavern near Colean house, called the Cove of Colean; which, as
well as Cassilis Downans, is famed, in country story, for being a favorite
haunt of fairies.-R.B.

4: The famous family of that name, the ancestors of Robert, the great
deliverer of his country, were Earls of Carrick.-R.B.

5: The first ceremony of Halloween is pulling each a "stock," or plant of
kail. They must go out, hand in hand, with eyes shut, and pull the first they
meet with: its being big or little, straight or crooked, is prophetic of the size
and shape of the grand object of all their spells the husband or wife. If any
"yird," or earth, stick to the root, that is "tocher," or fortune; and the taste
of the "custock," that is, the heart of the stem, is indicative of the natural
temper and disposition. Lastly, the stems, or, to give them their ordinary
appellation, the "runts," are placed somewhere above the head of the door;
and the Christian names of the people whom chance brings into the house

are, according to the priority of placing the "runts," the names in question.-R.B.

6: They go to the barnyard, and pull each, at three different times, a stalk of oats. If the third stalk wants the "top-pickle," that is, the grain at the top of the stalk, the party in question will come to the marriage-bed anything but a maid.-R.B.

7: When the corn is in a doubtful state, by being too green or wet, the stack-builder, by means of old timber, etc., makes a large apartment in his stack, with an opening in the side which is fairest exposed to the wind: this he calls a "fause-house."-R.B.

8: Burning the nuts is a favorite charm. They name the lad and lass to each particular nut, as they lay them in the fire; and according as they burn quietly together, or start from beside one another, the course and issue of the courtship will be.-R.B.

9: Whoever would, with success, try this spell, must strictly observe these directions: Steal out, all alone, to the kiln, and darkling, throw into the "pot" a clue of blue yarn; wind it in a new clue off the old one; and, toward the latter end, something will hold the thread: demand, "Wha hauds?" i.e., who holds? and answer will be returned from the kiln-pot, by naming the Christian and surname of your future spouse.-R.B.

10: Take a candle and go alone to a looking-glass; eat an apple before it, and some traditions say you should comb your hair all the time; the face of your conjungal companion, to be, will be seen in the glass, as if peeping over your shoulder.-R.B.

11: Steal out, unperceived, and sow a handful of hemp-seed, harrowing it with anything you can conveniently draw after you.
Repeat now and then: "Hemp-seed, I saw thee, hemp-seed, I saw thee; and him (or her) that is to be my true love, come after me and pou thee." Look over your left shoulder, and you will see the appearance of the person invoked, in the attitude of pulling hemp. Some traditions say, "Come after me and shaw thee," that is, show thyself; in which case, it simply appears. Others omit the harrowing, and say: "Come after me and harrow thee."-R.B.

12: This charm must likewise be performed unperceived and alone. You go to the barn, and open both doors, taking them off the hinges, if possible; for there is danger that the being about to appear may shut the doors, and do you some mischief. Then take that instrument used in winnowing the corn, which in our country dialect we call a "wecht," and go through all the attitudes of letting down corn against the wind. Repeat it three times, and the third time an apparition will pass through the barn, in at the windy door and out at the other, having both the figure in question, and the appearance or retinue, marking the employment or station in life.-R.B.

13: Take an opportunity of going unnoticed to a "bear-stack," and fathom it three times round. The last fathom of the last time you will catch in your arms the appearance of your future conjugal yoke-fellow.-R.B.

14: You go out, one or more (for this is a social spell), to a south running spring, or rivulet, where "three lairds' lands meet," and dip your left shirt sleeve. Go to bed in sight of a fire, and hang your wet sleeve before it to dry. Lie awake, and, some time near midnight, an apparition, having the exact figure of the grand object in question, will come and turn the sleeve, as if to dry the other side of it.-R.B.

15: Take three dishes, put clean water in one, foul water in another, and leave the third empty; blindfold a person and lead him to the hearth where the dishes are ranged; he (or she) dips the left hand; if bychance in the clean water, the future (husband or) wife will come tothe bar of matrimony a maid; if in the foul, a widow; if in the empty dish, it foretells, with equal certainty, no marriage at all. It is repeated three times, and every time the arrangement of the dishes is altered.-R.B.

16: Sowens, with butter instead of milk to them, is always the Halloween Supper.-R.B.

Handsome Nell

Tune– "I am a man unmarried."

ONCE I lov'd a bonie lass,
 Ay, and I love her still;
And whilst that virtue warms my breast,
 I'll love my handsome Nell.

As bonie lasses I hae seen,
 And mony full as braw;
But, for a modest gracefu' mein,
 The like I never saw.

A bonie lass, I will confess,
 Is pleasant to the e'e;
But, without some better qualities,
 She's no a lass for me.

But Nelly's looks are blythe and sweet,
 And what is best of a',
Her reputation is complete,
 And fair without a flaw.

She dresses aye sae clean and neat,
 Both decent and genteel;
And then there's something in her gait
 Gars ony dress look weel.

A gaudy dress and gentle air
 May slightly touch the heart;
But it's innocence and modesty
 That polishes the dart.

'Tis this in Nelly pleases me,
 'Tis this enchants my soul;
For absolutely in my breast
 She reigns without control.

Hark! The Mavis

Tune – "Ca' the yowes to the knowes."

Chorus.

Ca' the yowes to the knowes,
Ca' them where the heather grows
Ca' them where the burnie rows,
    My bonie dearie.

HARK! the mavis' evening sang
Sounding Cluden's woods amang,
Then a faulding let us gang,
    My bonie dearie.
        Ca' the, &c.

We'll gae down by Clouden side,
Thro' the hazels spreading wide,
O'er the waves that sweetly glide
    To the moon sae clearly.
        Ca' the, &c.

Yonder Clouden's silent towers,
Where at moonshine midnight hours,
O'er the dewy-bending flowers,
    Fairies dance sae cheery.
        Ca' the, &c.

Ghaist nor bogle shalt thou fear;
Thou 'rt to love and Heaven sae dear,
Nocht of ill may come thee near,
    My bonie dearie.
        Ca' the, &c.

Fair and lovely as thou art,
Thou hast stown my very heart;
I can die—but canna part,
    My bonie dearie.
        Ca' the, &c.

Here's To Thy Health

Tune – "Laggan Burn."

HERE'S to thy health, my bonie lass,
  Gude nicht and joy be wi' thee;
I'll come nae mair to thy bower door,
  To tell thee that I lo'e thee.
O dinna think, my pretty pink,
  But I can live without thee:
I vow and swear I dinna care,
  How lang ye look about ye.

Thou'rt aye sae free informing me,
  Thou hast nae mind to marry;
I'll be as free informing thee,
  Nae time hae I to tarry:
I ken thy friends try ilka means
  Frae wedlock to delay thee;
Depending on some higher chance –
  But fortune may betray thee.

I ken they scom my low estate,
  But that does never grieve me;
For I'm as free as any he;
  Sma' siller will relieve me.
I'll count my health my greatest wealth,
  Sa'e lang as I'll enjoy it;
I'll fear nae scant, I'll bode nae want,
  As lang's I get employment.

But far off fowls hae feathers fair,
  And, aye until ye try them:
Tho' they seem fair, still have a care,
  They may prove as bad a I am.
But at twal at night, when the moon shines bright,
  My dear, I'll come and see thee;
For the man that loves his mistress weel,
  Nae travel makes him weary.

Highland Mary

YE banks, and braes, and streams around
    The castle o' Montgomery,
Green be your woods and fair your flowers,
    Your waters never drumlie!
There simmer first unfauld her robes,
    And there the langest tarry;
For there I took the last fareweel,
    O' my sweet Highland Mary.

How sweetly bloom'd the gay green birk,
    How rich the hawthorn's blossom,
As underneath their fragrant shade
    I clasp'd her to my bosom!
The golden hours, on angel wings,
    Flew o'er me and my dearie;
For dear to me as light and life,
    Was my sweet Highland Mary.

Wi' monie a vow and lock'd embrace
    Our parting was fu' tender;
And, pledging aft to meet again,
    We tore oursels asunder;
But O! fell death's untimely frost,
    That nipt my flower sae early!
Now green's the sod, and cauld's the clay,
    That wraps my Highland Mary!

O pale, pale now, those rosy lips,
    I aft hae kiss'd sae fondly!
And closed for aye the sparkling glance,
    That dwelt on me sae kindly!
And mould'ring now in silent dust,
    That heart that lo'ed me dearly!
But still within my bosom's core
    Shall live my Highland Mary.

The Holy Fair

A note of seeming truth and trust
  Hid crafty Observation;
And secret hung, with poison'd crust,
  The dirk of Defamation:
A mask that like the gorget show'd
  Dye-varying, on the pigeon;
And for a mantle large and broad,
  He wrapt him in Religion.

HYPOCRISY-À-LA-MODE

UPON a simmer Sunday morn,
  When Nature's face is fair,
I walked forth to view the corn
  An' snuff the caller air.
The risin' sun, owre Galston muirs
  Wi' glorious light was glintin;
The hares were hirplin down the furrs,
  The lav'rocks they were chantin
    Fu' sweet that day.

As lightsomely I glowr'd abroad
  To see a scene sae gay,
Three Hizzies, early at the road,
  Cam skelpin up the way.
Twa had manteeles o' dolefu' black,
  But ane wi' lyart linin;
The third, that gaed a wee a-back,
  Was in the fashion shining
    Fu' gay that day.

The twa appear'd like sisters twin
  In feature, form, an' claes;
Their visage wither'd, lang an' thin,
  An' sour as ony slaes.
The third cam up, hap-step-an'-lowp,
  As light as ony lambie,
An' wi' a curchie low did stoop,
  As soon as e'er she saw me,
    Fu' kind that day.

Wi' bonnet aff, quoth I, "Sweet lass,
    I think ye seem to ken me;
I'm sure I've seen that bonie face,
    But yet I canna name ye."
Quo' she, an' laughin as she spak,
    An' taks me by the han's,
"Ye, for my sake, hae gien the feck
    Of a' the ten comman's
        A screed some day.

"My name is Fun — your cronie dear,
    The nearest friend ye hae;
An' this is Superstition here,
    An' that's Hypocrisy.
I'm gaun to Mauchline Holy Fair,
    To spend an hour in daffin:
Gin ye'll go there, you runkl'd pair,
    We will get famous laughin
        At them this day."

Quoth I, "With a' my heart, I'll do't:
    I'll get my Sunday's sark on,
An' meet you on the holy spot;
    Faith, we'se hae fine remarkin!"
Then I gaed hame at crowdie-time
    An' soon I made me ready;
For roads were clad frae side to side
    Wi' monie a wearie body
        In droves that day.

Here, farmers gash, in ridin graith,
    Gaed hoddin by their cotters,
There swankies young, in braw braidclaith
    Are springin owre the gutters.
The lasses, skelpin barefit, thrang,
    In silks an' scarlets glitter,
Wi' sweet-milk cheese in mony a whang,
    An' farls, bak'd wi' butter,
        Fu' crump that day.

When by the plate we set our nose,
    Weel heaped up wi' ha'pence,
A greedy glowr Black Bonnet throws,
    An' we maun draw our tippence.
Then in we go to see the show:
    On ev'ry side they're gath'rin,
Some carryin dails, some chairs an' stools,
    An' some are busy bleth'rin
        Right loud that day.

Here some are thinkin on their sins,
    An' some upo' their claes;
Ane curses feet that fyl'd his shins,
    Anither sighs an' prays:
On this hand sits a chosen swatch,
    Wi' screw'd-up grace-proud faces;
On that a set o' chaps at watch,
    Thrang winkin on the lasses
        To chairs that day.

O happy is that man and blest!
    Nae wonder that it pride him!
Whase ain dear lass that he likes best,
    Comes clinkin down beside him!
Wi' arm repos'd on the chair back,
    He sweetly does compose him;
Which by degrees slips round her neck,
    An's loof upon her bosom,
        Unken'd that day.

Now a' the congregation o'er
    Is silent expectation;
For Moodie speels the holy door,
    Wi' tidings o' salvation.
Should Hornie, as in ancient days,
    'Mang sons o' God present him,
The vera sight o' Moodie's face
    To's ain het hame had sent him
        Wi' fright that day.

Hear how he clears the points o' faith
    Wi' rattlin an' wi' thumpin!
Now meekly calm, now wild in wrath
    He's stampin, an' he's jumpin!
His lengthen'd chin, his turn'd-up snout,
    His eldritch squeal and gestures,
Oh, how they fire the heart devout
    Like cantharidian plaisters,
        On sic a day!

But hark! the tent has chang'd its voice:
    There's peace and rest nae langer;
For a' the real judges rise,
    They canna sit for anger.
Smith opens out his cauld harangues,
    On practice and on morals;
An' aff the godly pour in thrangs,
    To gie the jars an' barrels
        A lift that day.

What signifies his barren shine
    Of moral pow'rs and reason?
His English style an' gesture fine
    Are a' clean out o' season.
Like Socrates or Antonine
    Or some auld pagan heathen,
The moral man he does define,
    But ne'er a word o' faith in
        That's right that day.

In guid time comes an antidote
    Against sic poison'd nostrum;
For Peebles, frae the water-fit,
    Ascends the holy rostrum:
See, up he's got the word o' God
    An' meek an' mim has view'd it,
While Common Sense has ta'en the road,
    An's aff, an' up the Cowgate
        Fast, fast that day.

Wee Miller niest the Guard relieves,
    An' Orthodoxy raibles,
Tho' in his heart he weel believes
    An' thinks it auld wives' fables:
But faith! the birkie wants a Manse,
    So cannilie he hums them;
Altho' his carnal wit an' sense
    Like hafflins-wise o'ercomes him
        At times that day.

Now butt an' ben the change-house fills
    Wi' yill-caup commentators:
Here's cryin out for bakes an gills,
    An' there the pint-stowp clatters;
While thick an' thrang, an' loud an' lang,
    Wi' logic an' wi' Scripture,
They raise a din, that in the end
    Is like to breed a rupture
        O' wrath that day.

Leeze me on drink! it gies us mair
    Than either school or college
It kindles wit, it waukens lear,
    It pangs us fou o' knowledge.
Be't whisky-gill or penny-wheep,
    Or ony stronger potion,
It never fails, on drinkin deep,
    To kittle up our notion
        By night or day.

The lads an' lasses, blythely bent
    To mind baith saul an' body,
Sit round the table weel content,
    An' steer about the toddy,
On this ane's dress an' that ane's leuk
    They're makin observations;
While some are cozie i' the neuk,
    An' forming assignations
        To meet some day.

But now the Lord's ain trumpet touts,
    Till a' the hills rae rairin,
An' echoes back return the shouts—
    Black Russell is na sparin.
His piercing words, like highlan' swords,
    Divide the joints an' marrow;
His talk o' hell, whare devils dwell,
    Our vera "sauls does harrow"
        Wi' fright that day!

A vast, unbottom'd, boundless pit,
    Fill'd fou o' lowin brunstane,
Whase ragin flame, an' scorching heat
    Wad melt the hardest whun-stane!
The half-asleep start up wi' fear
    An' think they hear it roarin,
When presently it does appear
    'Twas but some neibor snorin,
        Asleep that day.

'Twad be owre lang a tale to tell,
    How mony stories past,
An' how they crouded to the yill,
    When they were a' dismist:
How drink gaed round in cogs an' caups
    Amang the furms an' benches:
An' cheese and bred frae women's laps
    Was dealt about in lunches
        An' dawds that day.

In comes a gausie, gash guidwife
    An' sits down by the fire,
Syne draws her kebbuck an' her knife;
    The lasses they are shyer:
The auld guidmen, about the grace
    Frae side to side they bother,
Till some ane by his bonnet lays,
    And gi'es them't like a tether
        Fu' lang that day.

Waesucks! for him that gets nae lass,
    Or lasses that hae naething!
Sma' need has he to say a grace,
    Or melvie his braw clathing!
O wives, be mindfu' ance yoursel
    How bonie lads ye wanted,
An' dinna for a kebbuck-heel
    Let lasses be affronted
        On sic a day!

Now Clinkumbell, wi' rattlin tow,
    Begins to jow an' croon;
Some swagger hame the best they dow,
    Some wait the afternoon.
At slaps the billies halt a blink,
    Till lasses strip their shoon:
Wi' faith an' hope, an' love an' drink,
    They're a' in famous tune
        For crack that day.

How monie hearts this day converts
    O' sinners and o' lasses
Their hearts o' stane, gin night, are gane
    As saft as ony flesh is.
There's some are fou o' love divine,
    There's some are fou o' brandy;
An' monie jobs that day begin,
    May end in houghmagandie
        Some ither day.

Holy Willie's Prayer

O Thou, wha in the heavens does dwell,
Who, as it pleases best thysel',
Sends ane to heaven an' ten to hell,
    A' for thy glory,
And no for ony gude or ill
    They've done afore thee!

I bless and praise thy matchless might,
When thousands thou hast left in night,
That I am here afore thy sight,
    For gifts an' grace
A burning and a shining light
    To a' this place.

What was I, or my generation,
That I should get sic exaltation?
I wha deserve sic just damnation
    For broken laws,
Five thousand years ere my creation,
    Thro' Adam's cause.

When frae my mither's womb I fell,
Thou might hae plunged me in hell,
To gnash my gums, to weep and wail,
    In burnin' lakes,
Where damned devils roar and yell,
    Chain'd to a stake.

Yet I am here a chosen sample,
To show thy grace is great and ample;
I'm here a pillar in thy temple,
    Strong as a rock,
A guide, a buckler, and example,
    To a' thy flock.

O Lord, thou kens what zeal I bear,
When drinkers drink, and swearers swear,
And singin there, and dancin here,
    Wi' great an' sma';
For I am keepit by thy fear
    Free frae them a'.

But yet, O Lord! confess I must,
At times I'm fash'd wi' fleshly lust:
An' sometimes, too, wi' wardly trust,
    Vile self gets in:
But Thou remembers we are dust,
    Defil'd in sin.

O Lord! yestreen, Thou kens, wi' Meg –
Thy pardon I sincerely beg,
O! may't ne'er be a livin plague
    To my dishonour,
An' I'll ne'er lift a lawless leg
    Again upon her.

Besides, I farther maun allow,
Wi' Leezie's lass, three times I trow;
But Lord, that Friday I was fou,
    When I cam near her;
Or else, thou kens, thy servant true
    Wad ne'er hae steer'd her.

May be thou lets this fleshly thorn
Beset thy servant e'en and morn,
Lest he owre proud and high should turn,
    That he's sae gifted;
If sae, thy hand maun e'en be borne,
    Until thou lift it.

Lord, bless thy chosen in this place,
For here Thou hast a chosen race;
But God confound their stubborn face,
    And blast their name,
Wha bring thy elders to disgrace
    An' public shame.

Lord, mind Gawn Hamilton's deserts;
He drinks, an' swears, an' plays at cartes,
Yet has sae mony takin arts,
    Wi' great an' sma',
Frae God's ain priest the people's hearts
    He steals awa?

An' when we chasten'd him therefore,
Thou kens how he bred sic a splore,
As set the warld in a roar
    O' laughing at us;
Curse Thou his basket and his store,
    Kail and potatoes.

Lord, hear my earnest cry an' pray'r,
Against that presbyt'ry o' Ayr;
Thy strong right hand, Lord, make it bare,
    Upo' their heads;
Lord visit them, and dinna spare,
    For their misdeeds.

O Lord my God, that glib-tongu'd Aiken,
My very heart and flesh are quakin,
To think how we stood sweatin, shakin,
    An' p—'d wi' dread,
While he, wi' hingin lip an' snakin',
    Held up his head.

Lord, in the day o' vengeance try him,
Lord, visit them wha did employ him,
And pass not in thy mercy by 'em,
    Nor hear their pray'r:
But for thy people's sake, destroy 'em,
    An' dinna spare.

But, Lord, remember me an' mine
Wi' mercies temp'ral and divine,
That I for grace and gear may shine,
    Excell'd by nane,
An' a' the glory shall be thine,
    Amen, Amen!

How Cruel Are the Parents

Tune – "John Anderson, my Jo."

HOW cruel are the parents
    Who riches only prize,
And to the wealthy booby
    Poor woman sacrifice!
Meanwhile, the hapless daughter
    Has but a choice of strife;
To shun a tyrant father's hate-
    Become a wretched wife.

The ravening hawk pursuing,
    The trembling dove thus flies,
To shun impelling ruin,
    Awhile her pinions tries;
Till, of escape despairing,
    No shelter or retreat,
She trusts the ruthless falconer,
    And drops beneath his feet.

I Dream'd I Lay . . .

I DREAMED I lay where flowers were springing
    Gaily in the sunny beam;
List'ning to the wild birds singing,
    By a failing crystal stream:
Straight the sky grew black and daring;
    Thro' the woods the whirlwinds rave;
Trees with aged arms were warring,
    O'er the swelling drumlie wave.

Such was my life's deceitful morning,
    Such the pleasures I enjoyed:
But lang or noon, loud tempests storming
    A' my flowery bliss destroy'd.
Tho' fickle fortune has deceiv'd me,
    She promis'd fair, and perform'd but ill;
Of mony a joy and hope bereav'd me;
    I bear a heart shall support me still.

In The Character of A Ruined Farmer

Tune –"Go from my window, Love, do."

THE sun he is sunk in the west,
All creatures retired to rest,
While here I sit, all sore beset,
    With sorrow, grief, and woe:
And it's O, fickle Fortune, O!

The prosperous man is asleep,
Nor hears how the whirlwinds sweep;
But Misery and I must watch
    The surly tempest blow:
And it's O, fickle Fortune, O!

There lies the dear partner of my breast;
Her cares for a moment at rest:
Must I see thee, my youthful pride,
    Thus brought so very low!
And it's O, fickle Fortune, O!

There lie my sweet babies in her arms;
No anxious fear their little hearts alarms;
But for their sake my heart does ache,
    With many a bitter throe:
And it's O, fickle Fortune, O!

I once was by Fortune carest:
I once could relieve the distrest:
Now life's poor support, hardly earn'd
    My fate will scarce bestow:
And it's O, fickle Fortune, O!

No comfort, no comfort I have!
How welcome to me were the grave!
But then my wife and children dear –
    O, whither would they go!
And it's O, fickle Fortune, O!

O whither, O whither shall I turn!
All friendless, forsaken, forlorn!
For, in this world, Rest or Peace
    I never more shall know!
And it's O, fickle Fortune, O!

It Was A' For Our Rightfu' King

IT was a' for our rightfu' King
    That we left fair Scotland's strand;
It was a' for our rightfu' King
    We e'er saw Irish land,
        My dear;
    We e'er saw Irish land.

Now a' is done that men can do,
    And a' is done in vain;
My love, and native land farewell!
    For I maun cross the main,
        My dear;
    For I maun cross the main.

He turn'd him right and round about,
    Upon the Irish shore,
He gave his bridle-reins a shake,
    With adieu for evermore,
        My dear;
    With adieu for evermore!

The sodger from the war returns,
    The sailor frae the main.
But I hae parted frae my love,
    Never to meet again,
        My dear;
    Never to meet again.

When day is gane and night is come,
    And a' folk bound to sleep,
I think on him that's far awa',
    The lee-lang night, and weep,
        My dear;
    The lee-lang night, and weep.

John Barleycorn: A Ballad

THERE was three kings into the east,
    Three kings both great and high,
And they, hae sworn a solemn oath
    John Barleycorn should die.

They took a plough and plough'd him down,
    Put clods upon his head,
And they hae sworn a solemn oath
    John Barleycorn was dead.

But the cheerful Spring came kindly on,
    And show'rs began to fall;
John Barleycorn got up again,
    And sore surpris'd them all.

The sultry suns of Summer came,
    And he grew thick and strong;
His head weel arm'd wi' point'd spears,
    That no one should him wrong.

The sober Autumn enter'd mild,
    When he grew wan and pale;
His bending joints and drooping head
    Show'd he began to fall.

His colour sicken'd more and more,
    He faded into age;
And then his enemies began
    To show their deadly rage.

They've taen a weapon, long and sharp,
    And cut him by the knee;
Then tied him fast upon a cart,
    Like a rogue for forgerie.

They laid him down upon his back,
    And cudgell'd him full sore;
They hung him up before the storm,
    And turned him o'er and o'er.

They filled up a darksome pit
    With water to the brim;
They heaved in John Barleycorn,
    There let him sink or swim.

They laid him out upon the floor,
    To work him farther woe;
And still, as signs of life appear'd,
    They toss'd him to and fro,

They wasted, o'er a scorching flame,
    The marrow of his bones;
But a miller us'd him worst of all,
    For he crushd him between two stones.

And they hae taen his very heart's blood,
    And drank it round and round;
And still the more and more they drank,
    Their joy did more abound.

John Barleycorn was a hero bold,
    Of noble enterprise;
For if you do but taste his blood,
    'Twill make your courage rise.

'Twill make a man forget his woe;
    'Twill heighten all his joy;
'Twill make the widow's heart to sing,
    Tho' the tear were in her eye.

Then let us toast John Barleycorn,
    Each man a glass in hand;
And may his great posterity
    Ne'er fail in old Scotland!

The Jolly Beggars: A Cantata

Recitativo

When lyart leaves bestrow the yird,
Or wavering like the bauckie-bird,
    Bedim cauld Boreas' blast;
When hailstanes drive wi' bitter skyte,
And infant frosts begin to bite,
    In hoary cranreuch drest;
Ae night at e'en a merry core
O' randie, gangrel bodies,
    In Poosie-Nansie's held the splore,
To drink their orra duddies;
Wi' quaffing an' laughing,
    They ranted an' they sang,
Wi' jumping an' thumping,
The vera girdle rang,

First, neist the fire, in auld red rags,
Ane sat, weel brac'd wi' mealy bags,
    And knapsack a' in order;
His doxy lay within his arm;
Wi' usquebae an' blankets warm
    She blinkit on her sodger;
An' aye he gies the tozie drab
The tither skelpin kiss,
    While she held up her greedy gab,
Just like an aumous dish;
Ilk smack still, did crack still,
    Just like a cadger's whip;
Then staggering an' swaggering
He roar'd this ditty up –

Air
Tune – "Soldier's Joy."

I am a son of Mars who have been in many wars,
And show my cuts and scars wherever I come;
This here was for a wench, and that other in a trench,

When welcoming the French at the sound of the drum.
Lal de daudle, &c.

My prenticeship I past where my leader breath'd his
    last,
When the bloody die was cast on the heights of Abram:
And I served out my trade when the gallant game was
    play'd,
And the Moro low was laid at the sound of the drum.

I lastly was with Curtis among the floating batt'ries,
And there I left for witness an arm and a limb;
Yet let my country need me, with Elliot to head me,
I'd clatter on my stumps at the sound of a drum.

And now tho' I must beg, with a wooden arm and leg,
And many a tatter'd rag hanging over my bum,
I'm as happy with my wallet, my bottle, and my callet,
As when I used in scarlet to follow a drum.

What tho' with hoary locks, I must stand the winter
    shocks,
Beneath the woods and rocks oftentimes for a home,
When the t'other bag I sell, and the tother bottle tell,
I could meet a troop of hell, at the sound of a drum.

Recitativo

He ended; and the kebars sheuk,
Aboon the chorus roar;
While frighted rattons backward leuk,
An' seek the benmost bore:
A fairy fiddler frae the neuk,
He skirl'd out, encore!
But up arose the martial chuck,
An' laid the loud uproar.

Tune-"Sodger Laddie."

I once was a maid, tho' I cannot tell when,
And still my delight is in proper young men;
Some one of a troop of dragoons was my daddie,
No wonder I'm fond of a sodger laddie,
Sing, lal de lal, &c.

The first of my loves was a swaggering blade,
To rattle the thundering drum was his trade;
His leg was so tight, and his cheek was so ruddy,
Transported I was with my sodger laddie.

But the godly old chaplain left him in the lurch;
The sword I forsook for the sake of the church:
He ventur'd the soul, and I risked the body,
'Twas then I proved false to my sodger laddie.

Full soon I grew sick of my sanctified sot,
The regiment at large for a husband I got;
From the gilded spontoon to the fife I was ready,
I asked no more but a sodger laddie.

But the peace it reduc'd me to beg in despair,
Till I met old boy in a Cunningham fair,
His rags regimental, they flutter'd so gaudy,
My heart it rejoic'd at a sodger laddie.

And now I have liv'd – I know not how long,
And still I can join in a cup and a song;
But whilst with both hands I can hold the glass steady,
Here's to thee, my hero, my sodger laddie.

Recitativo

Poor Merry-Andrew, in the neuk,
Sat guzzling wi' a tinkler-hizzie;
They mind't na wha the chorus teuk,
Between themselves they were sae busy:
At length, wi' drink an' courting dizzy,

He stoiter'd up an' made a face;
Then turn'd an' laid a smack on Grizzie,
Syne tun'd his pipes wi' grave grimace.

Air
Tune – "Auld Sir Symon."

Sir Wisdom's a fool when he's fou;
Sir Knave is a fool in a session;
He's there but a prentice I trow,
But I am a fool by profession.

My grannie she bought me a beuk,
An' I held awa to the school;
I fear I my talent misteuk,
But what will ye hae of a fool?

For drink I would venture my neck;
A hizzie's the half of my craft;
But what could ye other expect
Of ane that's avowedly daft?

I ance was tied up like a stirk,
For civilly swearing and quaffin;
I ance was abus'd i' the kirk,
For towsing a lass i' my daffin.

Poor Andrew that tumbles for sport,
Let naebody name wi' a jeer;
There's even, I'm tauld, i' the Court
A tumbler ca'd the Premier.

Observ'd ye yon reverend lad
Mak faces to tickle the mob;
He rails at our mountebank squad, –
It's rivalship just i' the job.

And now my conclusion I'll tell,
For faith I'm confoundedly dry;
The chiel that's a fool for himsel',
Guid Lord! he's far dafter than I.

Then niest outspak a raucle carlin,
Wha kent fu' weel to cleek the sterlin;
For mony a pursie she had hooked,
An' had in mony a well been douked:
Her love had been a Highland laddie,
But weary fa' the waefu' woodie!
Wi' sighs an' sobs she thus began
To wail her braw John Highlandman.

Air
Tune – "O, An Ye Were Dead, Guidman."

A Highland lad my love was born,
The Lalland laws he held in scorn;
But he still was faithfu' to his clan,
My gallant, braw John Highlandman.

Chorus.
Sing hey my braw John Highlandman!
Sing ho my braw John Highlandman!
There's not a lad in a' the lan'
Was match for my John Highlandman.

With his philibeg an' tartan plaid,
An' guid claymore down by his side,
The ladies' hearts he did trepan,
My gallant, braw John Highlandman.
Sing hey, &c.

We ranged a' from Tweed to Spey,
An' liv'd like lords an' ladies gay;
For a Lalland face he feared none, –
My gallant, braw John Highlandman.
Sing hey, &c.

They banish'd him beyond the sea.
But ere the bud was on the tree,
Adown my cheeks the pearls ran,
Embracing my John Highlandman.
Sing hey, &c.

But, och! they catch'd him at the last,
And bound him in a dungeon fast:
My curse upon them every one,
They've hang'd my braw John Highlandman!
Sing hey, &c.

And now a widow, I must mourn
The pleasures that will ne'er return:
The comfort but a hearty can,
When I think on John Highlandman.
Sing hey, &c.

Recitativo

A pigmy scraper wi' his fiddle,
Wha us'd at trystes an' fairs to driddle.
Her strappin limb and gausy middle
(He reach'd nae higher)
Had hol'd his heartie like a riddle,
An' blawn't on fire.

Wi' hand on hainch, and upward e'e,
He croon'd his gamut, one, two, three,
Then in an arioso key,
The wee Apoll
Set off wi' allegretto glee
His giga solo.

Air
Tune – "Whistle Owre the Lave O't."

Let me ryke up to dight that tear,
An' go wi' me an' be my dear;
An' then your every care an' fear
May whistle owre the lave o't.

Chorus.
I am a fiddler to my trade,
An' a' the tunes that e'er I played,
The sweetest still to wife or maid,
Was whistle owre the lave o't.

At kirns an' weddins we'se be there,
An' O sae nicely's we will fare!
We'll bowse about till Daddie Care
Sing whistle owre the lave o't.
I am, &c.

Sae merrily's the banes we'll pyke,
An' sun oursel's about the dyke;
An' at our leisure, when ye like,
We'll whistle owre the lave o't.
I am, &c.

But bless me wi' your heav'n o' charms,
An' while I kittle hair on thairms,
Hunger, cauld, an' a' sic harms,
May whistle owre the lave o't.
I am, &c.

Recitativo

Her charms had struck a sturdy caird,
As weel as poor gut-scraper;
He taks the fiddler by the beard,
An' draws a roosty rapier –
He swoor, by a' was swearing worth,
To speet him like a pliver,
Unless he would from that time forth
Relinquish her for ever.

Wi' ghastly e'e poor tweedle-dee
Upon his hunkers bended,
An' pray'd for grace wi' ruefu' face,
An' so the quarrel ended.
But tho' his little heart did grieve
When round the tinkler prest her,
He feign'd to snirtle in his sleeve,
When thus the caird address'd her:

Tune – "Clout the Cauldron."

My bonie lass, I work in brass,
A tinkler is my station:
I've travell'd round all Christian ground
In this my occupation;
I've taen the gold, an' been enrolled
In many a noble squadron;
But vain they search'd when off I march'd
To go an' clout the cauldron.
I've taen the gold, &c.

Despise that shrimp, that wither'd imp,
With a' his noise an' cap'rin;
An' take a share with those that bear
The budget and the apron!
And by that stowp! my faith an' houp,
And by that dear Kilbaigie,
If e'er ye want, or meet wi' scant,
May I ne'er weet my craigie.
And by that stowp, &c.

Recitativo

The caird prevail'd – th' unblushing fair
In his embraces sunk;
Partly wi' love o'ercome sae sair,
An' partly she was drunk:
Sir Violino, with an air
That show'd a man o' spunk,
Wish'd unison between the pair,
An' made the bottle clunk
To their health that night.

But hurchin Cupid shot a shaft,
That play'd a dame a shavie –
The fiddler rak'd her, fore and aft,
Behint the chicken cavie.
Her lord, a wight of Homer's craft,
Tho' limpin wi' the spavie,

He hirpl'd up, an' lap like daft,
An' shor'd them *Dainty Davie*
O' boot that night.

He was a care-defying blade
As ever Bacchus listed!
Tho' Fortune sair upon him laid,
His heart, she ever miss'd it.
He had no wish but – to be glad,
Nor want but – when he thirsted;
He hated nought but – to be sad,
An' thus the muse suggested
His sang that night.

Air
Tune – "For A' That, an' A' That."

I am a Bard of no regard,
Wi' gentle folks an' a' that;
But Homer-like, the glowrin byke,
Frae town to town I draw that.

Chorus.
For a' that, an' a' that,
An' twice as muckle's a' that;
I've lost but ane, I've twa behin',
I've wife eneugh for a' that.

I never drank the Muses' stank,
Castalia's burn, an' a' that;
But there it streams an' richly reams,
My Helicon I ca' that.
For a' that, &c.

Great love I bear to a' the fair,
Their humble slave an' a' that;
But lordly will, I hold it still
A mortal sin to thraw that.
For a' that, &c.
In raptures sweet, this hour we meet,
Wi' mutual love an' a' that;
But for how lang the flie may stang,

Let inclination law that.
For a' that, &c.

Their tricks an' craft hae put me daft,
They've taen me in, an' a' that;
But clear your decks, and here's – "The Sex!"
I like the jads for a' that.

Chorus.
For a' that, an' a' that,
An' twice as muckle's a' that;
My dearest bluid, to do them guid,
They're welcome till't for a' that.

Recitativo

So sang the bard – and Nansie's wa's
Shook with a thunder of applause,
Re-echo'd from each mouth!
They toom'd their pocks, they pawn'd their duds,
They scarcely left to co'er their fuds,
To quench their lowin drouth:
Then owre again, the jovial thrang
The poet did request
To lowse his pack an' wale a sang,
A ballad o' the best;
He rising, rejoicing,
Between his twa Deborahs,
Looks round him, an' found them
Impatient for the chorus.

Air
Tune - "Jolly Mortals, Fill your Glasses."

See the smoking bowl before us,
Mark our jovial ragged ring!
Round and round take up the chorus,
And in raptures let us sing –

A fig for those by law protected!
Liberty's a glorious feast!
Courts for cowards were erected,
Churches built to please the priest.

What is title, what is treasure,
What is reputation's care?
If we lead a life of pleasure,
'Tis no matter how or where!
A fig for, &c.

With the ready trick and fable,
Round we wander all the day;
And at night in barn or stable,
Hug our doxies on the hay.
A fig for, &c.

Does the train-attended carriage
Thro' the country lighter rove?
Does the sober bed of marriage
Witness brighter scenes of love?
A fig for, &c.

Life is all a variorum,
We regard not how it goes;
Let them cant about decorum,
Who have character to lose.
A fig for, &c.

Here's to budgets, bags and wallets!
Here's to all the wandering train.
Here's our ragged brats and callets,
One and all cry out, Amen!

The Lass of Cessnock Banks

A Song of Similes

Tune – "If he be a Butcher neat and trim."

ON Cessnock banks a lassie dwells;
    Could I describe her shape and mein;
Our lasses a' she far excels,
    An' she has twa sparkling rogueish een.

She's sweeter than the morning dawn,
    When rising Phoebus first is seen,
And dew-drops twinkle o'er the lawn;
    An' she has twa sparkling rogueish een.

She's stately like yon youthful ash,
    That grows the cowslip braes between,
And drinks the stream with vigour fresh;
    An' she has twa sparkling rogueish een.

She's spotless like the flow'ring thorn,
    With flow'rs so white and leaves so green,
When purest in the dewy morn;
    An' she has twa sparkling rogueish een.

Her looks are like the vernal May,
    When ev'ning Phoebus shines serene,
While birds rejoice on every spray;
    An' she has twa sparkling rogueish een.

Her hair is like the curling mist,
    That climbs the mountain-sides at e'en,
When flow'r-reviving rains are past;
    An' she has twa sparkling rogueish een.

Her forehead's like the show'ry bow,
    When gleaming sunbeams intervene
And gild the distant mountain's brow;
    An' she has twa sparkling rogueish een.

A Red, Red Rose

O, MY luve's like a red, red rose
    That's newly sprung in June:
O, My luve's like the melodie
    That's sweetly played in tune.

So fair art thou, my bonnie lass,
    So deep in love am I:
And I will luve thee still, my dear,
    Till a' the seas gang dry.

Till a' the seas gang dry, my dear,
    And the rocks melt with the sun:
And I will luve thee still, my dear,
    While the sands o' life shall run.

And fare thee weel, my only luve.
    And fare thee weel awhile!
And I will come again, my luve,
    Tho' it were ten thousand mile.

Love in the Guise of Friendship

YOUR friendship much can make me blest,
    O why that bliss destroy!
Why urge the only, one request
    You know I will deny!

Your thought, if Love must harbour there,
    Conceal it in that thought;
Nor cause me from my bosom tear
    The very friend I sought.

Man Was Made to Mourn: A Dirge

WHEN chill November's surly blast
    Made fields and forests bare,
One ev'ning, as I wander'd forth
    Along the banks of Ayr,
I spy'd a man, whose aged step
    Seem'd weary, worn with care;
His face was furrowd o'er with years,
    And hoary was his hair.

Young stranger, whither wand'rest thou?
    Began the rev'rend Sage;
Does thirst of wealth thy step constrain,
    Or youthful pleasure's rage?
Or haply, prest with cares and woes,
    Too soon thou hast began
To wander forth, with me to mourn
    The miseries of Man.

The sun that overhangs yon moors,
    Out-spreading far and wide,
Where hundreds labour to support
    A haughty lordling's pride;
I've seen you weary winter-sun
    Twice forty times return;
And ev'ry time has added proofs,
    That Man was made to mourn.

O man! while in thy early years,
    How prodigal of time!
Mis-spending all thy precious hours,
    Thy glorious, youthful prime!
Alternate follies take the sway;
    Licentious passions burn;
Which tenfold force gives Natures law,
    That Man was made to mourn.

Look not alone on youthful prime,
    Or manhood's active might;
Man then is useful to his kind,
    Supported is his right:
But see him on the edge of life,
    With cares and sorrows worn;
Then age and want, Oh! ill-match'd pair!
    Show Man was made to mourn.

A few seem favourites of fate,
    In pleasure's lap carest;
Yet, think not all the rich and great
    Are likewise truly blest:
But, Oh! what crowds in ev'ry land,
    All wretched and forlorn;
Thro' weary life this lesson learn,
    That Man was made to mourn.

Many and sharp the num'rous ills
    Inwoven with our frames!
More pointed still we make ourselves
    Regret, remorse, and shame!
And man, whose heaven-erected face
    The smiles of love adorn,
Man's inhumanity to man
    Makes countless thousands mourn!

See yonder poor, o'erlabour'd wight,
    So abject, mean, and vile,
Who begs a brother of the earth
    To give him leave to toil;
And see his lordly fellow-worm
    The poor petition spurn,
Unmindful, tho' a weeping wife
    And helpless offspring mourn.

If I'm design'd yon lordling's slave,
    By nature's law design'd,
Why was an independent wish
    E'er planted in my mind?

If not, why am I subject to
    His cruelty or scorn?
Or why has man the will and pow'r
    To make his felow mourn?

Yet, let not this too much, my son,
    Disturb thy youthful breast:
This partial view of human-kind
    Is surely not the last!
The poor, opressed, honest man
    Had never, sure, been born,
Had there not been some recompense
    To comfort those that mourn!

O Death! the poor man's dearest friend,
    The kindest and the best!
Welcome the hour my aged limbs
    Are laid with thee at rest!
The great, the wealthy fear thy blow
    From pomp and pleasure torn;
But, oh! a blest relief for those
    That weary-laden mourn!

Mary Morison

Tune – "Bide Ye Yet."

O MARY, at thy window be,
    It is the wisli'd, the trysted hour!
Those smiles and glances let me see,
    That make the miser's treasure poor:
How blythely wad I bide the stoure,
    A weary slave frae sun to sun,
Could I the rich reward secure,
    The lovely Mary Morison.

Yestreen, when to the trembling string
    The dance gaed thro' the lighted ha',
To thee my fancy took its wing,
    I sat, but neither heard nor saw:
Tho' this was fair, and that was braw,
    And yon the toast of a' the town,
I sigh'd, and said among them a',
    "Ye are na Mary Morison."

Oh, Mary, canst thou wreck his peace,
    Wha for thy sake wad gladly die?
Or canst thou break that heart of his,
    Whase only faut is loving thee?
If love for love thou wilt na gie,
    At least be pity to me shown;
A thought ungentle canna be
    The thought o' Mary Morison.

Montgomerie's Peggy

Tune – "Galla Water."

ALTHO' my bed were in yon muir,
　　Amang the heather, in my plaidie;
Yet happy, happy would I be,
　　Had I my dear Montgomerie's Peggy.

When o'er the hill beat surly storms,
　　And winter nights were dark and rainy;
I'd seek some dell, and in my arms
　　I'd shelter dear Montgomerie's Peggy.

Were I a Baron proud and high,
　　And horse and servants waiting ready;
Then a' 'twad gie o' joy to me,
　　The sharin't with Montgomerie's Peggy.

O Leave Novels

O LEAVE novels, ye Mauchline belles,
    Ye're safer at your spinning wheel;
Such witching books are baited hooks
    For rakish rooks like Rob Mossgiel;

Your fine Tom Jones and Grandisons,
    They make your youthful fancies reel;
They heat your brains, and fire your veins,
    And then you're prey for Rob Mossgiel.

Beware a tongue that's smoothly hung,
    A heart that warmly seems to feel;
That feeling heart but acts a part,
    'Tis rakish art in Rob Mossgiel.

The frank address, the soft caress,
    Are worse than poison'd darts of steel;
The frank address, and politesse,
    Are all finesse in Rob Mossgiel.

The Ordination

For sense, they little owe to frugal Heav'n –
To please the mob, they hide the little giv'n.

KILMARNOCK Wabsters, fidge an' claw,
  An' pour your creeshie nations;
An' ye wha leather rax an' draw,
  Of a' denominations;
Swith to the Laigh Kirk, ane an' a'
  An' there tak up your stations;
Then aff to Begbie's in a raw,
  An' pour divine libations
    For joy this day.

Curst Common-sense, that imp o' hell,
  Cam in wi' Maggie Lauder;
But Oliphant aft made her yell,
  An' Russell sair misca'd her:
This day Mackinlay taks the flail,
  An' he's the boy will blaud her!
He'll clap a shangan on her tail,
  An' set the bairns to daud her
    Wi' dirt this day.

Mak haste an' turn King David owre,
  And lilt wi' holy clangor;
O' double verse come gie us four,
  An' skirl up the Bangor:
This day the kirk kicks up a stoure,
  Nae mair the knaves shall wrang her,
For Heresy is in her pow'r,
  And gloriously she'll whang her
    Wi' pith this day.

Come, let a proper text be read,
    An' touch it aff wi' vigour,
How graceless Ham leugh at his dad,
    Which made Canaan a niger;
Or Phineas drove the murdering blade,
    Wi' whore-abhorring rigour;
Or Zipporah, the scauldin jad,
    Was like a bluidy tiger
        I' th' Inn that day.

There, try his mettle on the creed,
    An' bind him down wi' caution,
That Stipend is a carnal weed
    He takes by for the fashion;
And gie him o'er the flock, to feed,
    And punish each transgression;
Especial, rams that cross the breed,
    Gie them sufficient threshin;
        Spare them nae day.

Now, auld Kilmarnock, cock thy tail,
    An' toss thy horns fu' canty;
Nae mair thou'lt rowt out-owre the dale,
    Because thy pasture's scanty;
For lapfu's large o' gospel kail
    Shall fill thy crib in plenty,
An' runts o' grace the pick an' wale,
    No gi'en by way o' dainty,
        But ilka day.

Nae mair by Babel streams we'll weep,
    To think upon our Zion;
And hing our fiddles up to sleep,
    Like baby-clouts a-dryin:
Come, screw the pegs wi' tunefu' cheep,
    And o'er the thairms be tryin;
Oh, rare to see our elbucks wheep,
    And a' like lamb-tails flyin
        Fu' fast this day.

Lang, Patronage, with rod o' airn,
    Has shor'd the Kirk's undoin;
As lately Fenwick, sair forfairn,
    Has proven to its ruin:
Our patron, honest man! Glencairn,
    He saw mischief was brewin;
An' like a godly, elect bairn,
    He's wal'd us out a true ane,
        And sound this day.

Now Robertson harangue nae mair,
    But steek your gab for ever;
Or try the wicked town of Ayr,
    For there they'll think you clever;
Or, nae reflection on your lear,
    Ye may commence a Shaver;
Or to the Netherton repair,
    An' turn a Carpet-weaver
        Aff-hand this day.

Mutrie and you were just a match,
    We never had sic twa drones;
Auld Hornie did the Laigh Kirk watch,
    Just like a winkin baudrons:
And aye he catch'd the tither wretch,
    To fry them in his caudrons;
But now his Honour maun detach,
    Wi' a' his brimstone squadrons,
        Fast, fast this day.

See, see auld Orthodoxy's faes
    She's swingein thro' the city!
Hark, how the nine-tail'd cat she plays!
    I vow it's unco pretty!
There, Learning, with his Greekish face,
    Grunts out some Latin ditty;
And Common-sense is gaun, she says,
    To mak to Jamie Beattie
        Her plaint this day.

But there's Morality himsel,
   Embracing all opinions;
Hear, how he gies the tither yell,
   Between his twa companions!
See, how she peels the skin an' fell,
   As ane were peelin onions!
Now there, they're packed aff to hell,
   An' banish'd our dominions,
      Henceforth this day.

O happy day! rejoice, rejoice!
   Come bouse about the porter!
Morality's demure decoys
   Shall here nae mair find quarter:
M'Kinlay, Russell, are the boys
   That heresy can torture;
They'll gie her on a rape a hoyse,
   And cowe her measure shorter
      By th' head some day.

Come, bring the tither mutchkin in,
   And here's-for a conclusion,
To ev'ry New Light mother's son,
   From this time forth, Confusion!
If mair they deave us wi' their din,
   Or Patronage intrusion,
We'll light a spunk, and ev'ry skin,
   We'll rin them aff in fusion
      Like oil, some day.

Paraphrase of the First Psalm

THE man, in life wherever plac'd,
    Hath happiness in store,
Who walks not in the wicked's way,
    Nor learns their guilty lore:

Nor from the seat of scornful pride
    Casts forth his eyes abroad,
But with humility and awe
    Still walks before his God.

That man shall flourish like the trees,
    Which by the streamlets grow;
The fruitful top is spread on high,
    And firm the root below.

But he whose blossom buds in guilt
    Shall to the ground be cast,
And, like the rootless stubble tost,
    Before the sweeping blast.

For why? that God the good adore,
    Hath giv'n them peace and rest,
But hath decreed that wicked men
    Shall ne'er be truly blest.

The Parting Kiss

HUMID seal of soft affections,
   Tend'rest pledge of future bliss,
Dearest tie of young connections,
   Love's first snow drop, virgin kiss.

Speaking silence, dumb confession,
   Passion's birth, and infants' play,
Dove-like fondness, chaste concession,
   Glowing dawn of future day!

Sorrowing joy, Adieu's last action,
   (Ling'ring lips must now disjoin),
What words can ever speak affection
   Thrilling and sincere as thine!

The Ploughman's Life

As I was a-wand'ring ae morning in spring,
I heard a young ploughman sae sweetly to sing;
And as he was singin', thir words he did say, –
There's nae life like the ploughman's in the month o' sweet May.

The lav'rock in the morning she'll rise frae her nest,
And mount i' the air wi' the dew on her breast,
And wi' the merry ploughman she'll whistle and sing,
And at night she'll return to her nest back again.

Poem On Pastoral Poetry

Hail, Poesie! thou Nymph reserv'd!
In chase o' thee, what crowds hae swerv'd
Frae common sense, or sunk enerv'd
    'Mang heaps o' clavers;
And och! o'er aft thy joes hae starv'd,
    'Mid a' thy favours!

Say, Lassie, why, thy train amang,
While loud the trump's heroic clang,
And sock or buskin skelp alang
    To death or marriage;
Scarce ane has tried the shepherd-sang
    But wi' miscarriage?

In Homer's craft Jock Milton thrives;
Eschylus' pen Will Shakespeare drives;
Wee Pope, the knurlin', till him rives
    Horatian fame;
In thy sweet sang, Barbauld, survives
    Even Sappho's flame.

But thee, Theocritus, wha matches?
They're no herd's ballats, Maro's catches;
Squire Pope but busks his skinklin' patches
    O' heathen tatters:
I pass by hunders, nameless wretches,
    That ape their betters.

In this braw age o' wit and lear,
Will nane the Shepherd's whistle mair
Blaw sweetly in its native air,
    And rural grace;
And, wi' the far-fam'd Grecian, share
    A rival place?

Yes! there is ane; a Scottish callan —
There's ane; come forrit, honest Allan!
Thou need na jouk behint the hallan,
    A chiel sae clever;
The teeth o' Time may gnaw Tantallan,
    But thou's for ever.

Thou paints auld Nature to the nines,
In thy sweet Caledonian lines;
Nae gowden stream thro' myrtle twines,
    Where Philomel,
While nightly breezes sweep the vines,
    Her griefs will tell!

In gowany glens thy burnie strays,
Where bonie lasses bleach their claes,
Or trots by hazelly shaws and braes,
    Wi' hawthorns gray,
Where blackbirds join the shepherd's lays,
    At close o' day.

Thy rural loves are Nature's sel';
Nae bombast spates o' nonsense swell;
Nae snap conceits, but that sweet spell
    O' witchin love;
That charm that can the strongest quell,
    The sternest move.

A Poet's Welcome To His Love-Begotten Daughter

THE FIRST INSTANCE THAT ENTITLED HIM TO THE VENERABLE APPELATION OF A FATHER

THOU's welcome, wean; mishanter fa' me,
If thoughts o' thee, or yet thy mamie,
Shall ever daunton me or awe me,
   My bonie lady,
Or if I blush when thou shalt ca' me
   Tyta or daddie.

Tho' now they ca' me fornicator,
An' tease my name in kintry clatter,
The mair they talk, I'm kent the better,
   E'en let them clash;
An auld wife's tongue's a feckless matter
   To gie ane fash.

Welcome! my bonie, sweet, wee dochter,
Tho' ye come here a wee unsought for,
And tho' your comin' I hae fought for,
   Baith kirk and queir;
Yet, by my faith ye're no unwrought for,
   That I shall swear!

Wee image o' my bonie Betty,
As fatherly I kiss and daut thee,
As dear, and near my heart I set thee
   Wi' as gude will
As a' the priests hald seen me get thee
   That's out o' h–ll.

Sweet fruit o' mony a merry dint,
My funny toil is now a' tint,
Sin' thou came to the warl' asklent,
   Which fools may scoff at;
In my last plack thy part's be in't
   The better ha'f o't.

Tho' I should be the waur bestead,
Thou's be as braw and bienly clad,
And thy young years as nicely bred
    Wi' education,
As ony brat o' wedlock's bed,
    In a' thy station.

Lord grant that thou may aye inherit
Thy mither's person, grace, an' merit,
An' thy poor, worthless daddy's spirit,
    Without his failins,
'Twill please me mair to see thee heir it,
    Than stockit mailens.

For if thou be what I wad hae thee,
And tak the counsel I shall gie thee,
I'll never rue my trouble wi' thee,
    The cost nor shame o't,
But be a loving father to thee,
    And brag the name o't.

A Prayer in the Prospect of Death

O THOU unknown, Almighty Cause
  Of all my hope and fear!
In whose dread presence, ere an hour,
  Perhaps I must appear!

If I have wander'd in those paths
  Of life I ought to shun;
As something, loudly, in my breast,
  Remonstrates I have done;

Thou know'st that Thou hast form'd me
  With passions wild and strong;
And list'ning to their witching voice
  Has often led me wrong.

Where human weakness has come short,
  Or frailty stept aside,
Do Thou, All Good! for such Thou art ,
  In shades of darkness hide.

Where with intention I have err'd,
  No other plea I have,
But, Thou art good; and Goodness still
  Delighteth to forgive.

A Prayer Under the Pressure
of Violent Anguish

O THOU great Being! what Thou art,
    Surpasses me to know:
Yet sure I am, that known to Thee
    Are all Thy works below.

Thy creature here before Thee stands,
    All wretched and distrest;
Yet sure those ills that wring my soul
    Obey Thy high behest.

Sure, Thou, Almighty, canst not act
    From cruelty or wrath!
O, free my weary eyes from tears,
    Or close them fast in death!

But, if I must afflicted be,
    To suit some wise design;
Then man my soul with firm resolves,
    To bear and not repine!

Remorse – A Fragment

OF all the numerous ills that hurt our peace,
That press the soul, or wring the mind with anguish
Beyond comparison the worst are those
By our own folly, or our guilt brought on:
In ev'ry other circumstance, the mind
Has this to say, "it was no deed of mine:"
But, when to all the evil of misfortune
This sting is added, "blame thy foolish self!"
Or worser far, the pangs of keen remorse,
The torturing, gnawing consciousness of guilt –
Of guilt, perhaps, when we've involved others,
The young, the innocent, who fondly lov'd us;
Nay more, that very love their cause of ruin!
O burning hell! In all thy store of torments
There's not a keener lash!
Lives there a man so firm, who, while his heart
Feels all the bitter horrors of his crime,
Can reason down its agonizing throbs;
    And, after proper purpose of amendment,
Can firmly force his jarring thoughts to peace?
O happy, happy, enviable man!
O glorious magnanimity of soul!

The Rights of Woman

AN OCCASIONAL ADDRESS. SPOKEN BY MISS FONTENELLE
ON HER BENEFIT NIGHT, NOVEMBER 26, 1792.

While Europe's eye is fix'd on mighty things,
The fate of Empires and the fall of Kings;
While quacks of State must each produce his plan,
And even children lisp the Rights of Man;
Amid this mighty fuss just let me mention,
The Rights of Woman merit some attention.

First, in the Sexes' intermix'd connection,
One sacred Right of Woman is, Protection. –
The tender flower that lifts its head, elate,
Helpless, must fall before the blasts of Fate,
Sunk on the earth, defac'd its lovely form,
Unless your shelter ward th' impending storm.

Our second Right – but needless here is caution,
To keep that right inviolate's the fashion;
Each man of sense has it so full before him,
He'd die before he'd wrong it – 'tis Decorum.
There was, indeed, in far less polish'd days,
A time, when rough rude man had naughty ways;
Would swagger, swear, get drunk, kick up a riot,
Nay even thus invade a Lady's quiet!
Now, thank our stars! those Gothic times are fled;
Now, well-bred men – and you are all well-bred!
Most justly think (and we are much the gainers)
Such conduct neither spirit, wit, nor manners.

For Right the third, our last, our best, our dearest,
That Right to fluttering female hearts the nearest;
Which even the Rights of Kings, in low prostration,
Most humbly own – 'tis dear, dear admiration!
In that blest sphere alone we live and move;
There taste that life of life – immortal love. –
Sighs, fears, smiles, glances, fits, flirtations, airs;
'Gainst such an host what flinty savage dares –

When awful Beauty joins with all her charms,
Who is so rash as rise in rebel arms?

Then truce with kings, and truce with constitutions,
With bloody armaments and revolutions!
Let Majesty your first attention summon,
Ah! ça ira! THE MAJESTY OF WOMAN!

A Rose-Bud By My Early Walk

Tune – "The Shepherd's Wife."

A ROSE-BUD by my early walk,
Adown a corn-enclosed bawk,
Sae gently bent its thorny stalk,
    All on a dewy morning.

Ere twice the shades o' dawn are fled,
In a' its crimson glory spread,
And drooping rich the dewy head,
    It scents the early morning.

Within the bush her covert nest
A little linnet fondly prest,
The dew sat chilly on her breast
    Sae early in the morning.

She soon shall see her tender brood,
The pride, the pleasure o' the wood,
Amang the fresh green leaves bedew'd,
    Awake the early morning.

So thou, dear bird, young Jeany fair,
On trembling string or vocal air,
Shall sweetly pay the tender care
    That tents thy early morning.

So thou, sweet rose-bud, young and gay,
Shalt beauteous blaze upon the day,
And bless the parent's evening ray
    That watch'd thy early morning.

Sappho Redivivus – A Fragment

By all I lov'd, neglected and forgot,
No friendly face e'er lights my squalid cot;
Shunn'd, hated, wrong'd, unpitied, unredrest,
The mock'd quotation of the scorner's jest!
Ev'n the poor support of my wretched life,
Snatched by the violence of legal strife.
Oft grateful for my very daily bread
To those my family's once large bounty fed;
A welcome inmate at their homely fare,
My griefs, my woes, my sighs, my tears they share:
(Their vulgar souls unlike the souls refin'd,
The fashioned marble of the polished mind).

In vain would Prudence, with decorous sneer,
Point out a censuring world, and bid me fear;
Above the world, on wings of Love, I rise –
I know its worst, and can that worst despise;
Let Prudence' direst bodements on me fall,
M[ontgomer]y, rich reward, o'erpays them all!

Mild zephyrs waft thee to life's farthest shore,
Nor think of me and my distress more, –
Falsehood accurst! No! still I beg a place,
Still near thy heart some little, little trace:
For that dear trace the world I would resign:
O let me live, and die, and think it mine!

"I burn, I burn, as when thro' ripen'd corn
By driving winds the crackling flames are borne;"
Now raving-wild, I curse that fatal night,
Then bless the hour that charm'd my guilty sight:
In vain the laws their feeble force oppose,
Chain'd at Love's feet, they groan, his vanquish'd foes.
In vain Religion meets my shrinking eye,
I dare not combat, but I turn and fly:
Conscience in vain upbraids th' unhallow'd fire,
Love grasps her scorpions – stifled they expire!
Reason drops headlong from his sacred throne,

Your dear idea reigns, and reigns alone;
Each thought intoxicated homage yields,
And riots wanton in forbidden fields.
By all on high adoring mortals know!
By all the conscious villain fears below!
By your dear self! – the last great oath I swear,
Not life, nor soul, were ever half so dear!

Scotch Drink

Gie him strong drink until he wink,
　　That's sinking in despair;
An' liquor guid to fire his bluid,
　　That's prest wi' grief and care:
There let him bouse, an' deep carouse,
　　Wi' bumpers flowing o'er,
Till he forgets his loves or debts,
　　An' minds his griefs no more.
　　　　　　　SOLOMON'S PROVERBS, XXXI. 6, 7.

LET other Poets raise a fracas
'Bout vines, an' wines, an' drunken Bacchus,
An' crabbit names an' stories wrack us,
　　An' grate our lug,
I sing the juice Scotch bear can mak us,
　　In glass or jug.

O thou, my Muse! guid auld Scotch drink!
Whether thro' wimplin worms thou jink,
Or, richly brown, ream owre the brink,
　　In glorious faem,
Inspire me, till I lisp an' wink,
　　To sing thy name!

Let husky Wheat the haughs adorn,
An' Aits set up their awnie horn,
An' Pease and Beans, at een or morn,
　　Perfume the plain:
Leeze me on thee, John Barleycorn,
　　Thou King o' grain!

On thee aft Scotland chows her cood,
In souple scones, the wale o' food!
Or tumblin in the boiling flood
　　Wi' kail an' beef;
But when thou pours thy strong heart's blood,
　　There thou shines chief.

Food fills the wame, an' keeps us livin;
Tho' life's a gift no worth receivin,
When heavy-dragg'd wi' pine an' grievin;
    But oil'd by thee,
The wheels o' life gae down-hill, scrievin,
    Wi' rattlin glee.

Thou clears the head o'doited Lear;
Thou cheers ahe heart o' drooping Care;
Thou strings the nerves o' Labour sair,
    At's weary toil;
Though even brightens dark Despair
    Wi' gloomy smile.

Aft, clad in massy, siller weed,
Wi' gentles thou erects thy head;
Yet, humbly kind in time o' need,
    The poor man's wine,
His weep drap parritch, or his bread,
    Thou kitchens fine.

Thou art the life o' public haunts;
But thee, what were our fairs and rants?
Ev'n godly meetings o' the saunts,
    By thee inspir'd,
When gaping they besiege the tents,
    Are doubly fir'd.

That merry night we get the corn in!
O sweetly, then, thou reams the horn in!
Or reekin on a New-Year mornin
    In cog or bicker,
An' just a wee drap sp'ritual burn in,
    An' gusty sucker!

When Vulcan gies his bellows breath,
An' ploughmen gather wi' their graith,
O rare! to see thee fizz an freath
    I' th' luggit caup!
Then Burnewin comes on like Death
    At ev'ry chap.

Nae mercy, then, for airn or steel;
The brawnie, banie, ploughman chiel,
Brings hard owrehip, wi' sturdy wheel,
    The strong forehammer,
Till block an' studdie ring an reel,
    Wi' dinsome clamour.

When skirlin weanies see the light,
Thou maks the gossips clatter bright,
How fumblin' cuifs their dearies slight,
    Wae worth the name!
Nae Howdie gets a social night,
    Or plack frae them.

When neibors anger at a plea,
An' just as wud as wud can be,
How easy can the barley-bree
    Cement the quarrel!
It's aye the cheapest Lawyer's fee,
    To taste the barrel.

Alake! that e'er my Muse has reason,
To wyte her countrymen wi' treason!
But mony daily weet their weason
    Wi' liquors nice,
An' hardly, in a winter season,
    E'er spier her price.

Wae worth that brandy, burnin trash!
Fell source o' mony a pain an' brash!
Twins mony a poor, doylt, drucken hash,
    O' half his days;
An' sends, beside, auld Scotland's cash
    To her warst faes.

Ye Scots, wha wish auld Scotland well,
Ye chief, to you my tale I tell,
Poor, plackless devils like mysel'
    It sets you ill,
Wi' bitter, dearthfu' wines to mell,
    Or foreign gill.

May gravels round his blather wrench,
An' gouts torment him, inch by inch,
What twists his gruntle wi' a glunch
    O' sour disdain,
Out owre a glass o' Whisky punch
    Wi' honest men!

O Whisky! soul o' plays an' pranks!
Accept a bardie's gratfu' thanks!
When wanting thee, what tuneless cranks
    Are my poor verses!
Thou comes–they rattle in their ranks,
    At ither's a——s!

Thee, Ferintosh! O sadly lost!
Scotland lament frae coast to coast!
Now colic-grips, an' barkin hoast
    May kill us a';
For loyal Forbes' charter'd boast
    Is ta'en awa?

Thae curst horse-leeches o' the' Excise,
Wha mak the Whisky Stells their prize!
Haud up thy han', Deil! ance, twice, thrice!
    There, seize the blinkers!
An' bake them up in brunstane pies
    For poor damn'd drinkers.

Fortune! if thou'll but gie me still
Hale breeks, a scone, an' Whisky gill,
An' rowth o' rhyme to rave at will,
    Tak a' the rest,
An' deal't about as thy blind skill
    Directs thee best.

Scots Wha Hae

Robert Bruce's Address to His Army.

Scots, wha hae wi' Wallace bled,
Scots, wham Bruce has aften led;
Welcome to your gory bed,
    Or to glorious victory!

Now's the day, and now's the hour;
See the front o' battle lower;
See approach proud Edward's power –
    Edward! chains and slavery!

Wha will be a traitor knave?
Wha can fill a coward's grave!
Wha sae base as be a slave?
    Traitor! coward! turn and flee!

Wha for Scotland's King and law
Freedom's sword will strongly draw,
Freeman stand, or freeman fa',
    Caledonian! on wi' me!

By oppression's woes and pains!
By your sons in servile chains!
We will drain our dearest veins,
    But they shall – they shall be free!

Lay the proud usurpers low!
Tyrants fall in every foe!
Liberty's in every blow!
    Forward! let us do or die!

Stanzas On Naething

Extempore Epistle To Gavin Hamilton, Esq.

To you, sir, this summons I've sent,
    Pray, whip till the pownie is freathing;
But if you demand what I want,
    I honestly answer you – naething.

Ne'er scorn a poor Poet like me,
    For idly just living and breathing,
While people of every degree
    Are busy employed about – naething.

Poor Centum-per-centum may fast,
    And grumble his hurdies their claithing,
He'll find, when the balance is cast,
    He's gane to the devil for – naething.

The courtier cringes and bows,
    Ambition has likewise its plaything;
A coronet beams on his brows;
    And what is a coronet? – naething.

Some quarrel the Presbyter gown,
    Some quarrel Episcopal graithing;
But every good fellow will own
    Their quarrel is a' about – naething.

The lover may sparkle and glow,
    Approaching his bonie bit gay thing:
But marriage will soon let him know
    He's gotten a buskit up naething.

The Poet may jingle and rhyme,
    In hopes of a laureate wreathing,
And when he has wasted his time,
    He's kindly rewarded with naething.

The thundering bully may rage,
 And swagger and swear like a heathen;
But collar him fast, I'll engage,
 You'll find that his courage is naething.

Last night wi' a feminine whig,
 A Poet she couldna put faith in;
But soon we grew lovingly big,
 I taught her, her terrors were naething.

Her whigship was wonderful pleased,
 But charmingly tickled wi' ae thing,
Her fingers I lovingly squeezed,
 And kissed her, and promised her – naething.

The priest anathemas may threat –
 Predicament, Sir, that we're baith in;
But when honour's reveille is beat,
 The holy artillery's naething.

And now I must mount on the wave,
 My voyage perhaps there is death in:
But what is a watery grave?
 The drowning a Poet is naething.

And now, as grim death's in my thought,
 To you, sir, I make this bequeathing:
My service as long as ye've ought,
 And my friendship, by God, when ye've naething.

Tam Glen

My heart is a breaking, dear Tittie,
    Some counsel unto me come len',
To anger them a' is a pity,
    But what will I do wi' Tam Glen?

I'm thinking, wi' sic a braw fellow,
    In poortith I might mak a fen:
What care I in riches to wallow,
    If I maunna marry Tam Glen?

There's Lowrie the Laird o' Dumeller,
    "Gude day to you, brute!" he comes ben:
He brags and he blaws o' his siller,
    But when will he dance like Tam Glen?

My minnie does constantly deave me,
    And bids me beware o' young men:
They flatter, she says, to deceive me,
    But wha can think sae o' Tam Glen?

My daddie says, gin I'll forsake him,
    He'd gie me gude hunder marks ten:
But, if it's ordain'd I maun take him,
    O wha will I get but Tam Glen?

Yestreen at the Valentine's dealing,
    My heart to my mou gied a sten:
For thrice I drew ane without failing,
    And thrice it was written Tam Glen!

The last Halloween I was waukin
    My droukit sark-sleeve, as ye ken;
His likeness came up the house staukin,
    And the very grey breeks o' Tam Glen!

Come, counsel, dear Tittie, don't tarry;
    I'll gie ye my bonie black hen,
Gif ye will advise me to marry
    The lad I lo'e dearly, Tam Glen.

Tam O' Shanter

A Tale

Of Brownyis and of Bogillis full is this Buke.
GAWIN DOUGLAS

WHEN chapman billies leave the street,
And drouthy neebors, neebors, meet,
As market days are wearing late,
And folk begin to tak the gate;
While we sit bousing at the nappy,
An' getting fou and unco happy,
We think na on the lang Scots miles,
The mosses, waters, slaps and styles,
That lie between us and our hame,
Where sits our sulky sullen dame,
Gathering her brows like gathering storm,
Nursing her wrath to keep it warm.

This truth fand honest Tam o' Shanter,
As he frae Ayr ae night did canter:
(Auld Ayr, wham ne'er a town surpasses,
For honest men and bonie lasses).

O Tam! had'st thou but been sae wise,
As taen thy ain wife Kate's advice!
She tauld thee weel thou was a skellum,
A blethering, blustering, drunken blellum;
That frae November till October,
Ae market-day thou was na sober;
That ilka melder wi' the miller,
Thou sat as lang as thou had siller;
That ev'ry naig was ca'd a shoe on
The Smith and thee gat roarin' fou on;
That at the Lord's house, ev'n on Sunday,
Thou drank wi' Kirton Jean till Monday,
She prophes'd that late or soon,
Thou wad be found, deep drown'd in Doon,
Or catch'd wi' warlocks in the mirk,
By Alloway's auld, haunted kirk.

Ah, gentle dames! it gars me greet,
To think how mony counsels sweet,
How mony lengthen'd, sage advices,
The husband frae the wife despises!

But to our tale: Ae market night,
Tam had got planted unco right,
Fast by an ingle, bleezing finely,
Wi' reaming swats, that drank divinely;
And at his elbow, Souter Johnny,
His ancient, trusty, drougthy crony:
Tam lo'ed him like a vera brither;
They had been fou for weeks thegither.
The night drave on wi' sangs an' clatter;
And aye the ale was growing better:
The Landlady and Tam grew gracious,
Wi' favours secret, sweet, and precious:
The Souter tauld his queerest stories;
The Landlord's laugh was ready chorus:
The storm without might rair and rustle,
Tam did na mind the storm a whistle.

Care, mad to see a man sae happy,
E'en drown'd himsel amang the nappy:
As bees flee hame wi' lades o' treasure,
The minutes wing'd their way wi' pleasure:
Kings may be blest, but Tam was glorious,
O'er a' the ills o' life victorious!

But pleasures are like poppies spread,
You seize the flow'r, its bloom is shed;
Or like the snow falls in the river,
A moment white – then melts for ever;
Or like the borealis race,
That flit ere you can point their place;
Or like the rainbow's lovely form
Evanishing amid the storm. –
Nae man can tether time nor tide,
The hour approaches Tam maun ride;
That hour, o' night's black arch the key-stane,
That dreary hour he mounts his beast in;

And sic a night he taks the road in,
As ne'er poor sinner was abroad in.

The wind blew as 'twad blawn its last;
The rattling showers rose on the blast;
The speedy gleams the darkness swallow'd;
Loud, deep, and lang, the thunder bellow'd:
That night, a child might understand,
The Deil had business on his hand.

Weel-mounted on his grey mare, Meg,
A better never lifted leg,
Tam skelpit on thro' dub and mire,
Despising wind, and rain, and fire;
Whiles holding fast his gude blue bonnet,
Whiles crooning o'er some auld Scots sonnet,
Whiles glow'rin round wi' prudent cares,
Lest bogles catch him unawares;
Kirk-Alloway was drawing nigh,
Where ghaists and houlets nightly cry. –

By this time he was cross the ford,
Where in the snaw the chapman smoor'd;
And past the birks and meikle stane,
Where drunken Charlie brak's neck-bane;
And thro' the whins, and by the cairn,
Whare hunters fand the murder'd bairn;
And near the thorn, aboon the well,
Where Mungo's mither hang'd hersel. –
Before him Doon pours all his floods;
The doubling storm roars thro' the woods;
The lightnings flash from pole to pole;
Near and more near the thunders roll:
When, glimmering thro' the groaning trees,
Kirk-Alloway seem'd in a bleeze,
Thro' ilka bore the beams were glancing,
And loud resounded mirth and dancing. –

Inspiring bold John Barleycorn!
What dangers thou canst make us scorn!
Wi' tippenny, we fear nae evil;

Wi' usquabae, we'll face the devil! –
The swats sae ream'd in Tammie's noddle,
Fair play, he car'd na deils a boddle,
But Maggie stood, right sair astonish'd,
Till, by the heel and hand admonish'd,
She ventur'd forward on the light;
And, vow! Tam saw an unco sight!
Warlocks and witches in a dance:
Nae cotillon brent new frae France,
But hornpipes, jigs, strathspeys, and reels,
Put life and mettle in their heels.
A winnock-bunker in the east,
There sat auld Nick, in shape o' beast;
A towzie tyke, black, grim, and large,
To gie them music was his charge:
He screw'd the pipes and gart them skirl,
Till roof and rafters a' did dirl. –
Coffins stood round, like open presses,
That shaw'd the Dead in their last dresses;
And by some devilish cantraip sleight
Each in its cauld hand held a light, –
By which heroic Tam was able
To note upon the haly table,
A murderer's banes in gibbet-airns;
Twa span-lang, wee, unchristen'd bairns;
A thief, new-cutted frae a rape,
Wi' his last gasp his gab did gape;
Five tomahawks, wi' blude red rusted:
Five scymitars, wi' murder crusted;
A garter which a babe had strangled:
A knife, a father's throat had mangled.
Whom his ain son o' life bereft,
The grey hairs yet stack to the heft;
Wi' mair of horrible and awfu',
Which even to name wad be unlawfu'.

As Tammie glowr'd, amaz'd, and curious,
The mirth and fun grew fast and furious:
The piper loud and louder blew;
The dancers quick and quicker flew;
The reel'd, they set, they cross'd, they cleekit,

Till ilka carlin swat and reekit,
And coost her duddies to the wark,
And linkit at it in her sark!

Now Tam, O Tam! had they been queans,
A' plump and strapping in their teens;
Their sarks, instead o' creeshie flainen,
Been snaw-white seventeen hunder linen!
Thir breeks o' mine, my only pair,
That ance were plush o' gude blue hair,
I wad hae gi'en them off my hurdies,
For ae blink o' the bonie burdies!

But wither'd beldams, auld and droll,
Rigwoodie hags wad spean a foal,
Lowping and flinging on a crummock,
I wonder did na turn thy stomach.

But Tam kent what was what fu' brawlie,
There was ae winsome wench and walie,
That night enlisted in the core,
(Lang after ken'd on Carrick shore;
For mony a beast to dead she shot,
And perish'd mony a bonie boat,
And shook baith meikle corn and bear,
And kept the country-side in fear);
Her cutty sark, o' Paisley harn,
That while a lassie she had worn,
In longitude tho' sorely scanty,
It was her best, and she was vauntie. –
Ah! little ken'd thy reverend grannie,
That sark she coft for her wee Nannie,
Wi' twa pund Scots ('twas a' her riches),
Wad ever grac'd a dance of witches!

But here my Muse her wing maun cour,
Sic flights are far beyond her pow'r;
To sing how Nannie lap and flang,
(A souple jade she was, and strang),
And how Tam stood, like ane bewitch'd,
And thought his very een enrich'd:

Even Satan glowr'd, and fidg'd fu' fain,
And hotch'd and blew wi' might and main:
Till first ae caper, syne anither,
Tam tint his reason a thegither,
And roars out, "Weel done, cutty-sark!"
And in an instant all was dark:
And scarcely had he Maggie rallied.
When out the hellish legion sallied.

As bees bizz out wi' angry fyke,
When plundering herds assail their byke;
As open pussie's mortal foes,
When, pop! she starts before their nose;
As eager runs the market-crowd,
When "Catch the thief!" resounds aloud;
So Maggie runs, the witches follow,
Wi' mony an eldritch skreech and hollow.

Ah, Tam! Ah, Tam! thou'll get thy fairin!
In hell, they'll roast thee like a herrin!
In vain thy Kate awaits thy comin!
Kate soon will be a woefu' woman!
Now, do thy speedy utmost, Meg,
And win the key-stone o' the brig:
There, at them thou thy tail may toss,
A running stream they dare na cross.
But ere the key-stane she could make,
The fient a tail she had to shake!
For Nannie, far before the rest,
Hard upon noble Maggie prest,
And flew at Tam wi' furious ettle;
But little wist she Maggie's mettle –
Ae spring brought off her master hale,
But left behind her ain grey tail:
The carlin claught her by the rump,
And left poor Maggie scarce a stump.

Now, wha this tale o' truth shall read,
Ilk man and mother's son, take heed;
Whene'er to drink you are inclin'd,
Or cutty-sarks rin in your mind,

Think ye may buy the joys o'er dear;
Remember Tam o' Shanter's mare.

Tam Samson's Elegy

An honest man's the noblest work of God.
POPE.

Has auld Kilmarnock seen the Deil?
Or great M'Kinlay thrawn his heel?
Or Robinson again grown weel,
    To preach an' read?
"Na' waur than a'!" cries ilka chiel,
    "Tam Samson's dead!"

Kilmarnock lang may grunt an' grane,
An' sigh, an' sab, an' greet her lane,
An' cleed her bairns, man, wife, an' wean,
    In mourning weed;
To Death, she's dearly pay'd the kane-
    Tam Samson's dead!

The Brethren o' the mystic level
May hing their head in woefu' bevel,
While by their nose the tears will revel,
    Like ony bead;
Death's gien the Lodge an unco devel,
    Tam Samson's dead!

When Winter muffles up his cloak,
And binds the mire like a rock;
When to the loughs the Curlers flock,
    Wi' gleesome speed,
Wha will they station at the *cock*?
    Tam Samson's dead!

He was the king o' a' the Core,
To guard, or draw, or wick a bore,
Or up the rink like Jehu roar,
    In time o' need;
But now he lags on Death's *hog-score*,
    Tam Samson's dead!

Now safe the stately Sawmont sail,
And Trouts bedropp'd wi' crimson hail,
And Eels, weel kend for souple tail,
    And Geds for greed,
Since, dark in Death's *fish-creel*, we wail
    Tam Samson's dead!

Rejoice, ye birring Paitricks a';
Ye cootie Moorcocks, crousely craw;
Ye Maukins, cock your fud fu' braw
    Withouten dread;
Your mortal Fae is now awa';
    Tam Samson's dead!

That woefu' morn be ever mourn'd,
Saw him in shooting graith adorn'd,
While pointers round impatient burn'd,
    Frae couples freed;
But, Och! he gaed and ne'er return'd!
    Tam Samson's dead!

In vain auld age his body batters,
In vain the gout his ancles fetters,
In vain the burns cam down like waters,
    An acre braid!
Now ev'ry auld wife, greetin, clatters
    "Tam Samson's dead!"

Owre mony a weary hag he limpit,
An' aye the tither shot he thumpit,
Till coward Death behind him jumpit,
    Wi' deadly feide;
Now he proclaims wi' tout o' trumpet,
    Tam Samson's dead!

When at his heart he felt the dagger,
He reel'd his wonted bottle-swagger,
But yet he drew the mortal trigger,
    Wi' weel-aimed heed;
"Lord, five!" he cry'd, an' owre did stagger;
    Tam Samson's dead!

Ilk hoary hunter mourn'd a brither;
Ilk sportsman youth bemoan'd a father;
Yon auld gray stane, amang the heather,
    Marks out his head;
Whare Burns has wrote, in rhyming blether,
    "Tam Samson's dead!"

There, low he lies, in lasting rest;
Perhaps upon his mould'ring breast
Some spitefu' muirfowl bigs her nest
    To hatch and breed:
Alas! nae mair he'll them molest!
    Tam Samson's dead!

When August winds the heather wave,
And sportsmen wander by yon grave,
Three vollies let his mem'ry crave,
    O' pouther an' lead,
Till Echo answer frae her cave,
    "Tam Samson's dead!"

Heav'n rest his saul whare'er he be!
Is th' wish o' mony mae than me:
He had twa fauts, or maybe three,
    Yet what remead?
Ae social, honest man want we:
    Tam Samson's dead!

THE EPITAPH

TAM SAMSON'S weel-worn clay here lies,
    Ye canting zealots, spare him!
If honest worth in heaven rise,
    Ye'll mend or ye win near him.

PER CONTRA

GO, Fame, an' canter like a filly
Thro' a' the streets an' neuks o' Killie,
Tell ev'ry social, honest billie
    To cease his grievin';
For yet, unskaithed by Death's gleggullie,
      Tam Samson's livin'!

The Tarbolton Lasses

IF ye gae up to yon hill–tap,
    Ye'll there see bonie Peggy;
She kens her father is a laird,
    And she forsooth's a leddy.

There Sophy tight, a lassie bright,
    Besides a handsome fortune:
Wha canna win her in a night,
    Has little art in courting.

Gae down by Faile, and taste the ale,
    And tak a look o' Mysie;
She's dour and din, a deil within,
    But aiblins she may please ye.

If she be shy, her sister try,
    Yell maybe fancy Jenny,
If ye'll dispense wi' want o' sense –
    She kens hersel she's bonie.

As ye gae up by yon hillside,
    Speer in for bonie Bessy;
She'll gi'e ye a beck, and bid ye light,
    And handsomely address ye.

There's few sae bonie, nane sae guid,
    In a' King George' dominion;
If ye should doubt the truth o' this –
    It's Bessy's ain opinion!

Thou Gloomy December

ANCE mair I hail thee, thou gloomy December!
    Ance mair I hail thee wi' sorrow and care;
Sad was the parting thou makes me remember–
    Parting wi' Nancy, oh! ne'er to meet mair.
Fond lovers' parting is sweet, painful pleasure,
    Hope beaming mild on the soft parting hour;
But the dire feeling, O farewell for ever!
    Is anguish unmingl'd, and agony pure.

Wild as the winter now tearing the forest,
    Till the last leaf o' the summer is flown,
Such is the tempest has shaken my bosom,
    Till my last hope and last comfort is gone;
Still as I hail thee, thou gloomy December,
    Still shall I hail thee wi' sorrow and care;
For sad was the parting thou makes me remember,
    Parting wi' Nancy, oh, ne'er to meet mair.

To A Louse

On Seeing One On A Lady's Bonnet, At Church

HA! whaur ye gaun, ye crowlin ferlie?
Your impudence protects you sairly;
I canna say but ye strunt rarely,
    Owre gauze and lace;
Tho', faith! I fear ye dine but sparely
    On sic a place.

Ye ugly, creepin, blastit wonner,
Detested, shunn'd by saunt an' sinner,
How daur ye set your fit upon her–
    Sae fine a lady?
Gae somewhere else and seek your dinner
    On some poor body.

Swith! in some beggar's haffet squattle;
There ye may creep, and sprawl, and sprattle,
Wi' ither kindred, jumping cattle,
    In shoals and nations;
Whaur horn nor bane ne'er daur unsettle
    Your thick plantations.

Now haud you there, ye're out o' sight,
Below the fatt'rels, snug and tight;
Na, faith ye yet! ye'll no be right,
    Till ye've got on it –
The verra tapmost, tow'rin height
    O' Miss's bonnet.

My sooth! right bauld ye set your nose out,
As plump an' grey as ony groset:
O for some rank, mercurial rozet,
    Or fell, red smeddum,
I'd gie you sic a hearty dose o't,
    Wad dress your droddum.

I wad na been surpris'd to spy
You on an auld wife's flainen toy;
Or aiblins some bit dubbie boy,
    On's wyliecoat;
But Miss' fine Lunardi! fye!
    How daur ye do't?

O Jeany, dinna toss your head,
An' set your beauties a' abread!
Ye little ken what cursed speed
    The blastie's makin:
Thae winks an' finger-ends, I dread,
    Are notice takin.

O wad some Power the giftie gie us
To see oursels as ithers see us!
It wad frae mony a blunder free us,
    An' foolish notion:
What airs in dress an' gait wad lea'e us,
    An' ev'n devotion!

To Mary In Heaven

Tune – "Miss Forbe's Farewell to Banff."

THOU ling'ring star, with lessening ray,
    That lov'st to greet the early morn,
Again thou usher'st in the day
    My Mary from my soul was torn.
O Mary! dear departed shade!
    Where is thy place of blissful rest?
See'st thou thy lover lowly laid?
    Hear'st thou the groans that rend his breast?

That sacred hour can I forget,
    Can I forget the hallow'd grove,
Where, by the winding Ayr, we met,
    To live one day of parting love?
Eternity will not efface
    Those records dear of transports past;
Thy image at our last embrace;
    Ah! little thought we 'twas our last!

Ayr, gurgling, kiss'd his pebbled shore,
    O'erhung with wild-woods, thickening green;
The fragrant birch and hawthorn hoar,
    'Twin'd amorous round the raptur'd scene,
The flowers sprang wanton to be prest,
    The birds sang love on ev'ry spray;
Till too, too soon, the glowing west,
    Proclaim'd the speed of winged day.

Still o'er these scenes my mem'ry wakes,
    And fondly broods with miser care!
Time but th' impression stronger makes,
    As streams their channels deeper wear.
My Mary! dear departed shade!
    Where is thy blissful place of rest?
See'st thou thy lover lowly laid?
    Hear'st thou the groans that rend his breast?

To A Mountain Daisy,

ON TURNING ONE DOWN WITH THE PLOUGH, IN APRIL, 1786

WEE, modest, crimson-tippèd flow'r,
Thou's met me in an evil hour;
For I maun crush amang the stoure
      Thy slender stem.
To spare thee now is past my pow'r,
      Thou bonie gem.

Alas! it's no thy neebor sweet,
The bonie Lark, companion meet!
Bending thee 'mang the dewy weet!
      Wi' spreckl'd breast,
When upward-springing, blythe, to greet
      The purpling east.

Cauld blew the bitter-biting north
Upon thy early, humble birth;
Yet cheerfully thou glinted forth
      Amid the storm,
Scarce rear'd above the parent-earth
      Thy tender form.

The flaunting flowers our gardens yield
High shelt'ring woods an' wa's maun shield:
But thou, beneath the random bield
      O' clod or stane,
Adorns the histie stibble-field,
      Unseen, alane.

There, in thy scanty mantle clad,
Thy snawie bosom sun-ward spread,
Thou lifts thy unassuming head
      In humble guise;
But now the share uptears thy bed,
      And low thou lies!

Such is the fate of artless Maid,
Sweet flow'ret of the rural shade!
By love's simplicity betray'd
  And guileless trust;
Till she, like thee, all soil'd, is laid
  Low i' the dust.

Such is the fate of simple Bard,
On life's rough ocean luckless starr'd!
Unskilful he to note the card
  Of prudent lore,
Till billows rage and gales blow hard,
  And whelm him o'er!

Such fate to suffering worth is giv'n,
Who long with wants and woes has striv'n,
By human pride or cunning driv'n
  To mis'ry's brink;
Till, wrench'd of ev'ry stay but Heav'n,
  He, ruin'd, sink!

Ev'n thou who mourn'st the Daisy's fate,
That fate is thine — no distant date;
Stern Ruin's ploughshare drives elate,
  Full on thy bloom,
Till crush'd beneath the furrow's weight,
  Shall be thy doom!

To A Mouse,

ON TURNING HER UP IN HER NEST WITH THE PLOUGH

WEE, sleekit, cow'rin, tim'rous beastie,
O, what a panic's in thy breastie!
Thou need na start awa sae hasty,
    Wi' bickering brattle!
I wad be laith to rin an' chase thee,
    Wi' murd'ring pattle!

I'm truly sorry man's dominion,
Has broken nature's social union,
An' justifies that ill opinion,
    Which makes thee startle
At me, thy poor, earth-born companion,
    An' fellow-mortal!

I doubt na, whiles, but thou may thieve;
What then? poor beastie, thou maun live!
A daimen-icker in a thrave
    'S a sma' request;
I'll get a blessin wi' the lave,
    An' never miss't!

Thy wee bit housie, too, in ruin!
It's silly wa's the win's are strewin!
An' naething, now, to big a new ane,
    O' foggage green!
An' bleak December's winds ensuin,
    Baith snell an' keen!

Thou saw the fields laid bare and waste,
An' weary winter comin fast,
An' cozie here, beneath the blast,
    Thou thought to dwell,
Till crash! the cruel coulter past,
    Out thro' thy cell.

That wee bit heap o' leaves an' stibble,
Has cost thee mony a weary nibble!
Now thou's turn'd out, for a' thy trouble,
    But house or hald,
To thole the winter's sleety dribble,
    An' cranreuch cauld!

But, Mousie, thou art no thy lane,
In proving foresight may be vain;
The best-laid schemes o' mice an 'men
    Gang aft agley,
An'lea'e us nought but grief an' pain,
    For promis'd joy.

Still thou art blest, compar'd wi' me!
The present only toucheth thee:
But, Och! I backward cast my e'e
    On prospects drear!
An' forward, tho' I canna see,
    I guess an' fear!

To Ruin

ALL hail! inexorable lord!
At whose destruction-breathing word,
   The mightiest empires fall!
Thy cruel, woe-delighted train,
The ministers of grief and pain,
   A sullen welcome, all!
With stern-resolv'd, despairing eye,
   I see each aimed dart;
For one has cut my dearest tie,
   And quivers in my heart.
      Then low'ring, and pouring,
        The storm no more I dread;
     Tho' thick'ning, and black'ning,
        Round my devoted head.

And thou grim pow'r, by life abhorr'd,
While life a pleasure can afford,
   Oh! hear a wretch's pray'r!
Nor more I shrink appall'd, afraid;
I court, I beg thy friendly aid,
   To close this scene of care!
When shall my soul, in silent peace,
   Resign life's joyless day-
My weary heart is throbbing cease,
   Cold mould'ring in the clay?
      No fear more, no tear more,
        To stain my lifeless face,
     Enclasped, and grasped,
        Within thy cold embrace!

Tragic Fragment

ALL villain as I am – a damned wretch,
A hardened, stubborn, unrepenting sinner,
Still my heart melts at human wretchedness;
And with sincere but unavailing sighs
I view the helpless children of distress:
With tears indignant I behold the oppressor
Rejoicing in the honest man's destruction,
Whose unsubmitting heart was all his crime –
Ev'n you, ye hapless crew! I pity you;
Ye, whom the seeming good think sin to pity;
Ye poor, despised, abandoned vagabonds,
Whom Vice, as usual, has turn'd o'er to ruin.
Oh I but for friends and interposing Heaven,
I had been driven forth like you forlorn,
The most detested, worthless wretch among you!
O injured God! Thy goodness has endow'd me
With talents passing most of my compeers,
Which I in just proportion have abused –
As far surpassing other common villains
As Thou in natural parts has given me more.

The Twa Dogs

A Tale

'TWAS in that place o' Scotland's isle,
That bears the name o' auld King Coil,
Upon a bonie day in June,
When wearin' thro' the afternoon,
Twa dogs, that were na thrang at hame,
Forgather'd ance upon a time.

The first I'll name, they ca'd him Caesar,
Was keepit for his Honor's pleasure:
His hair, his size, his mouth, his lugs,
Shew'd he was nane o' Scotland's dogs;
But whalpit some place far abroad,
Whare sailors gang to fish for Cod.

His locked, letter'd, braw brass collar
Shew'd him the gentleman and scholar;
But though he was o' high degree,
The fient a pride – nae pride had he;
But wad hae spent an hour caressin,
Ev'n wi' al tinkler-gipsey's messin.
At kirk or market, mill or smiddie,
Nae tawted tyke, tho' e'er sae duddie,
But he wad stan't, as glad to see him,
An' stroan't on stanes an' hillocks wi' him.

The tither was a ploughman's collie,
A rhyming, ranting, raving billie,
Wha for his friend and comrade had him,
And in freak had Luath ca'd him,
After some dog in Highland Sang,
Was made lang syne, – Lord knows how lang.

He was a gash an' faithfu' tyke,
As ever lap a sheugh or dyke.
His honest, sonsie, baws'nt face,
Aye gat him friends in ilka place;
His breast was white, his touzie back

Weel clad wi' coat o' glossy black;
His gawsie tail, wi' upward curl,
Hung owre his hurdie's wi' a swirl.

Nae doubt but they were fain o' ither,
And unco pack an' thick thegither;
Wi' social nose whyles snuff'd and snowkit;
Whiles mice an' moudieworts they howkit;
Whiles scour'd awa in lang excursion,
An' worry'd ither in diversion;
Until wi' daffin' weary grown,
Upon a knowe they set them down.
An' there began a lang digression.
About the lords o' the creation.

CAESAR

I've aften wonder'd, honest Luath,
What sort o' life poor dogs like you have;
An' when the gentry's life I saw,
What way poor bodies liv'd ava.

Our Laird gets in his racked rents,
His coals, his kane, an' a' his stents:
He rises when he likes himsel;
His flunkies answer at the bell;
He ca's his coach; he ca's his horse;
He draws a bonie silken purse,
As lang's my tail, where, thro' the steeks,
The yellow letter'd Geordie keeks.

Frae morn to e'en, it's nought but toiling,
At baking, roasting, frying, boiling;
An' tho' the gentry first are stechin,
Yet ev'n the ha' folk fill their pechan
Wi' sauce, ragouts, an' sic like trashtrie,
That's little short o' downright wastrie.
Our Whipper-in, wee blasted wonner,
Poor worthless elf, it eats a dinner,
Better than ony tenant man

His Honour has in a' the lan:
An' what poor cot-folk pit their painch in
I own it's past my comprehension.

LUATH

Trowth, Caesar, whiles they're fash't eneugh:
A cottar howkin in a sheugh,
Wi' dirty stanes biggin a dyke,
Baring a quarry, an' siclike;
Himsel, a wife, he thus sustains,
A smytrie o' wee duddie weans,
An' nought but his han' darg, to keep
Them right an' tight in thack an' rape.

An' when they meet wi' sair disasters,
Like loss o' health or want o' masters,
Ye maist wad think, a wee touch langer,
An' they maun starve o' cauld an' hunger,
But how it comes, I never kent yet,
They're maistly wonderfu' contented;
An' buirdly chiels, an' clever hizzies,
Are bred in sic a way as this is.

CAESAR

But then to see how ye're negleckit,
How huff'd, and cuff'd, and disrespeckit!
Lord man, our gentry care as little
For delvers, ditchers, an' sic cattle;
They gang as saucy by poor folk,
As I wad by a stinkin brock.

I've notic'd, on our Laird's court-day,
An' mony a time my heart's been wae,
Poor tenant bodies, scant o' cash,
How they maun thole a factor's snash:
He'll stamp an' threaten, curse an' swear
He'll apprehend them, poind their gear;
While they maun stan', wi' aspect humble,
An' hear it a', an' fear an' tremble!

I see how folk live that hae riches;
But surely poor-folk maun be wretches.

LUATH

They're no sae wretched's ane wad think:
Tho' constantly on poortith's brink,
They're sae accustom'd wi' the sight,
The view o't gies them little fright.

Then chance an' fortune are sae guided,
They're aye in less or mair provided;
An' tho' fatigued wi' close employment,
A blink o' rest's a sweet enjoyment.

The dearest comfort o' their lives,
Their grushie weans an' faithfu' wives:
The prattling things are just their pride,
That sweetens a' their fire-side.

An' whyles twalpennie worth o' nappy
Can mak the bodies unco happy:
They lay aside their private cares,
To mind the Kirk and State affairs;
They'll talk o' patronage an' priests,
Wi' kindling fury i' their breasts,
Or tell what new taxation's comin,
An' ferlie at the folk in Lon'on.

As bleak-fac'd Hallowmass returns,
They get the jovial, rantin kirns,
When rural life, of ev'ry station,
Unite in common recreation;
Love blinks, Wit slaps, an' social Mirth
Forgets there's Care upo' the earth.

That merry day the year begins,
They bar the door on frosty winds;
The nappy reeks wi' mantling ream,
An' sheds a heart-inspiring steam;
The luntin pipe, an' sneeshin mill,

Are handed round wi' right guid will;
The cantie auld folks crackin crouse,
The young anes rantin thro' the house, –
My heart has been sae fain to see them,
That I for joy hae barket wi' them.

Still it's owre true that ye hae said,
Sic game is now owre aften play'd.
There's monie a creditable stock
O' decent, honest, fawsont folk,
Are riven out baith root an' branch,
Some rascal's pridefu' greed to quench,
Wha thinks to knit himsel the faster
In favour wi' some gentle Master,
Wha, aiblins, thrang a parliamentin,
For Britain's guid his saul indentin –

CAESAR

Haith, lad, ye little ken about it:
For Britain's guid! guid faith! I doubt it.
Say rather, gaun as Premiers lead him:
An' saying *aye* or *no*'s they bid him:
At operas an' plays parading,
Mortgaging, gambling, masquerading:
Or maybe, in a frolic daft,
To Hague or Calais takes a waft,
To mak a tour an' tak a whirl,
To learn *bon ton*, an' see the worl'.

There, at Vienna, or Versailles,
He rives his father's auld entails;
Or by Madrid he takes the rout,
To thrum guitars an' fecht wi' nowt;
Or down Italian vista startles,
Whore-hunting amang groves o' myrtles:
Then bowses drumly German-water,
To mak himsel look fair and fatter,
An' clear the consequential sorrows,
Love-gifts of Carnival signoras.
For Britain's guid! for her destruction!

Wi' dissipation, feud, an' faction.

LUATH

Hech, man! dear sirs! is that the gate
They waste sae mony a braw estate?
Are we sae foughten an' harass'd
For gear to gang that gate at last?

O would they stay aback frae courts,
An' please themselves wi' countra sports,
It wad for ev'ry ane be better,
The Laird, the Tenant, and the Cotter!
For thae frank, rantin, ramblin, billies,
Fient haet o' them's ill-hearted fellows;
Except for breakin o' their timmer,
Or speakin lightly o' their limmer,
Or shootin of a hare or moor-cock,
The ne'er-a-bit they're ill to poor folk,

But will ye tell me, Master Caesar,
Sure great folk's life's a life o' pleasure?
Nae cauld nor hunger e'er can steer them,
The very thought o't need na fear them.

CAESAR

Lord, man, were ye but whyles whare I am,
The gentles, ye wad ne'er envy them!

It's true, they need na starve or sweat,
Thro' winter's cauld, or simmer's heat;
They've nae sair wark to craze their banes,
An' fill auld age wi' grips an' granes:
But human bodies are sic fools,
For a' their colleges and schools,
That when nae real ills perplex them,
They mak enow themselves to vex them;
An' aye the less they hae to sturt them,
In like proportion, less will hurt them.

A country fellow at the pleugh,
His acre's till'd, he's right eneugh;
A country girl at her wheel,
Her dizzen's dune, she's unco weel;
But Gentlemen, an' Ladies warst,
Wi' ev'n down want o' wark are curst.
They loiter, lounging, lank an' lazy;
Tho' deil haet ails them, yet uneasy;
Their days insipid, dull, an' tasteless;
Their nights unquiet, lang, an' restless;

An' ev'n their sports, their balls an' races,
Their galloping through public places,
There's sic parade, sic pomp, an' art,
The joy can scarcely reach the heart.

The men cast out in party-matches,
Then sowther a' in deep debauches.
Ae night they're mad wi' drink an' whoring,
Niest day their life is past enduring.
The Ladies arm-in-arm in clusters,
As great an' gracious a' as sisters;
But hear their absent thoughts o' ither,
They're a' run deils an' jads thegither.
Whyles, owre the wee bit cup an' platie,
They sip the scandal potion pretty;
Or lee-lang nights, wi' crabbit leuks
Pore owre the devil's pictur'd beuks;
Stake on a chance a farmer's stackyard,
An' cheat like ony unhang'd blackguard.

There's some exceptions, man an' woman;
But this is gentry's life in common.

By this, the sun was out of sight,
An' darker gloamin brought the night:
The bum-clock humm'd wi' lazy drone;
The kye stood rowtin i' the loan;
When up they gat an' shook their lugs,
Rejoic'd they were na *men* but *dogs*;
An' each took aff his several way,
Resolv'd to meet some ither day.

The Twa Herds

Blockheads with reason wicked wits abhor,
But Fool with Fool is barbarous civil war.
POPE

O A'YE pious godly flocks,
Weel fed on pastures orthodox,
Wha now will keep you frae the fox,
    Or worrying tykes?
Or wha will tent the waifs an' crocks,
    About the dykes?

The twa best herds in a' the wast,
The e'er ga'e gospel horn a blast,
These five an' twenty simmers past,
    Oh, dool to tell!
Hae had a bitter black out–cast
    Atween themsel.

O, Moodie, man, an' wordy Russel,
How could you raise so vile a bustle,
Ye'll see how new–light herds will whistle,
    An' think it fine!
The Lord's cause ne'er gat sic a twistle,
    Sin' I hae min'.

O, Sirs, whae'er wad hae expeckit,
Your duty ye wad sae negleckit,
Ye wha were ne'er by lairds respeckit
    To wear the plaid,
But by the brutes themselves eleckit,
    To be their guide.

What flock wi' Moodie's flock could rank,
Sae hale and hearty every shank
Nae poison'd soor Arminian's tank
    He let them taste,
Frae Calvin's well, aye clear, drank:
    O, sic a feast!

The thummart, willcat, brock, and tod,
Weel kend his voice thro' a' the wood,
He smell'd their ilka hole an' road,
    Baith out an in,
An' weel he lik'd to shed their bluid,
    An' sell their skin.

What herd like Russel tell'd his tale,
His voice was heard thro' muir and dale,
He kenn'd the Lord's sheep, ilka tail,
    Owre a' the height;
An' saw gin they were sick or hale,
    At the first sight.

He fine a mangy sheep could scrub,
Or nobly fling the gospel club,
And new-light herds could nicely drub,
    Or pay their skin;
Could shake them owre the burning dub,
    Or heave them in.

Sic twa – O! do I live to see't,
Sic famous twa should disagreet,
And names, like "villain," "hypocrite,"
    Ilk ither gi'en,
While New-Light herds, wi' laughin spite,
    Say "neither's liein"!

A' ye wha tent the gospel fauld,
There's Duncan deep, and Peebles shaul,
But chiefly thou, apostle Auld,
    We trust in thee,
That thou wilt work them, hot and cauld,
    Till they agree.

Consider, Sirs, how we're beset,
There's scarce a new herd that we get,
But comes frae 'mang that cursed set,
    I winna name,
I hope frae heav'n to see them yet
    In fiery flame.

Dalrymple has been lang our fae,
M'Gill has wrought us meikle wae,
And that curs'd rascal ca'd M'Quhae,
    And baith the Shaws,
That aft hae made us black an' blae,
    Wi' vengefu' paws.

Auld Wodrow lang has hatch'd mischief,
We thought aye death wad bring relief,
But he has gotten, to our grief,
    Ane to succeed him,
A chiel wha'll soundly buff our beef;
    I meikle dread him.

And monie a ane that I could tell,
Wha fain wad openly rebel,
Forby turn-coats amang oursel,
    There's Smith for ane,
I doubt he's but a grey nick quill,
    An' that ye'll fin'.

O! a' ye flocks owre a' the hills,
By mosses, meadows, moors, and fells,
Come join your counsel and your skills,
    To cowe the lairds,
An' get the brutes the power themsels
    To choose their herds.

Then Orthodoxy yet may prance,
An' Learning in a woody dance,
An' that fell cur ca'd Common Sense,
    That bites sae sair,
Be banished o'er the seas to France:
    Let him bark there.

Then Shaw's an' D'rymple's eloquence,
M'Gill's close nervous excellence
M'Quhae's pathetic manly sense,
    An' guid M'Math,
Wi' Smith, wha thro' the heart can glance,
    May a' pack aff.

A Vision

Tune – "Cummock Psalms."

As I stood by yon roofless tower,
    Where the wa'flower scents the dewy air,
Where the howlet mourns in her ivy bower,
    And tells the midnight moon her care;

Chorus..

A lassie, all alone was making her moan,
    Lamenting our lads beyond the sea:
In the Bluidy wars they fa', and our honour's gane
    an' a',
    And broken-hearted we maun die.

The winds were laid, the air was still,
    The stars they shot alang the sky;
The fox was howling on the hill,
    And the distant-echoing glens reply.

The stream, adown its hazelly path,
    Was rushing by the ruin'd wa's,
Hasting to join the sweeping Nith,
    Whase distant roaring swells and fa's.

The cauld blae North was streaming forth
    Her lights, wi' hissing, eerie din;
Athwart the lift they start and shift,
    Like Fortune's favors, tint as win.

By heedless chance I turn'd mine eyes,
    And, by the moonbeam, shook to see
A stern and stalwart ghaist arise,
    Attir'd as minstrels wont to be.

Had I a statue been o' stane,
    His daring look had daunted me;
And on his bonnet grav'd was plain,
    The sacred posy – Libertie!

And frae his harp sic strains did flow,
    Might rous'd the slumb'ring dead to hear;
But oh, it was a tale of woe,
    As ever met a Briton's ear!

He sang wi' joy his former day,
    He weeping wailed his latter times;
But what he said it was nae play,
    I winna venture't in my rhymes.

Where Are The Joys?

Where are the joys I have met in the morning,
   That danc'd to the lark's early song?
Where is the peace that awaited my wand'ring,
   At evening the wild woods among?

No more a winding the course of yon river,
   And marking sweet flowerets so fair,
No more I trace the light footsteps of pleasure,
   But sorrow and sad-sighing care.

Wae Is My Heart

WAE is my heart, and the tear's in my ee;
Lang, lang, joy's been a stranger to me:
Forsaken and friendless, my burden I bear,
And the sweet voice o' Pity ne'er sounds in my ear.

Love, thou hast pleasures; and deep hae I loved;
Love, thou hast sorrows; and sair hae I proved;
But this bruised heart that now bleeds in my breast,
I can feel its throbbings will soon be at rest.

Oh, if I were where happy I hae been;
Down by yon stream, and yon bonie castle green;
For there he is wand'ring and musing on me,
Wha wad soon dry the tear frae my Phillis's ee.

The Whistle: A Ballad

I SING of a Whistle, a Whistle of worth,
I sing of a Whistle, the pride of the North.
Was brought to the court of our good Scottish King,
And long with this Whistle all Scotland shall ring.

Old Loda, still rueing the arm of Fingal,
The god of the bottle sends down from his hall –
"This Whistle's your challenge, to Scotland get o'er,
And drink them to hell, Sir! or ne'er see me more!"

Old poets have sung, and old chronicles tell,
What champions ventur'd, what champions fell:
The son of great Loda was conqueror still,
And blew on the Whistle their requiem shrill.

Till Robert, the lord of the Cairn and the Scaur,
Unmatch'd at the bottle, unconquer'd in war,
He drank his poor god-ship as deep as the sea;
No tide of the Baltic e'er drunker than he.

Thus Robert, victorious, the trophy has gain'd;
Which now in his house has for ages remain'd;
Till three noble chieftains, and all of his blood,
The jovial contest again have renew'd.

Three joyous good fellows, with hearts clear of flaw;
Craigdarroch, so famous for with, worth, and law;
And trusty Glenriddel, so skill'd in old coins;
And gallant Sir Robert, deep-read in old wines.

Craigdarroch began, with a tongue smooth as oil,
Desiring Glenriddel to yield up the spoil;
Or else he would muster the heads of the clan,
And once more, in claret, try which was the man.

"By the gods of the ancients!" Glenriddel replies,
"Before I surrender so glorious a prize,
I'll conjure the ghost of the great Rorie More,
And bumper his horn with him twenty times o'er."

Sir Robert, a soldier, no speech would pretend,
But he ne'er turn'd his back on his foe – or his friend;
Said, toss down the Whistle, the prize of the field,
And, knee-deep in claret, he'd die ere he'd yield.

To the board of Glenriddel our heroes repair,
So noted for drowning of sorrow and care;
But, for wine and for welcome, not more known to
    fame,
Than the sense, wit, and taste, of a sweet lovely dame.

A bard was selected to witness the fray,
And tell future ages the feats of the day;
A Bard who detested all sadness and spleen,
And wish'd that Parnassus a vineyard had been.

The dinner being over, the claret they ply,
And ev'ry new cork is a new spring of joy;
In the bands of old friendship and kindred so set,
And the bands grew the tighter the more they were
    wet.

Gay Pleasure ran riot as bumpers ran o'er:
Bright Phoebus ne'er witness'd so joyous a core,
And vow'd that to leave them he was quite forlorn,
Till Cynthia hinted he'd see them next morn.

Six bottles a-piece had well wore out the night,
When gallant Sir Robert, to finish the fight,
Turn'd o'er in one bumper a bottle of red,
And swore 'twas the way that their ancestor did.

Then worthy Glenriddel, so cautious and sage,
No longer the warfare ungodly would wage;
A high-ruling elder to wallow in wine!
He left the foul business to folks less divine.

The gallant Sir Robert fought hard to the end;
But who can with Fate and quart bumpers contend?
Though Fate said, a hero should perish in light;
So uprose bright Phoebus – and down fell the knight.

Next up rose our bard, like a prophet in drink: –
"Craigdarroch, thou'lt soar when creation shall sink!
But if thou would flourish immortal in rhyme,
Come – one bottle more – and have at the sublime!

"Thy line, that have struggled for freedom with Bruce,
Shall heroes and patriots ever produce:
So thine be the laurel, and mine be the bay;
The field thou hast won, by yon bright god of day!"

Wilt Thou Be My Dearie?

A NEW SCOTS SONG.

Tune – "The Sutor's Dochter."

WILT thou be my Dearie?
When sorrow wring thy gentle heart
O wilt thou let me cheer thee?
By the treasure of my soul,
That's the love I bear thee!
I swear and vow that only thou
Shall ever be my dearie –
Only thou, I swear and vow,
Shall ever be my dearie!

Lassie, say thou lo'es me;
Or, if thou wilt na be my ain,
O say na thou'lt refuse me!
If it winna, canna be,
Thou for thine may choose me,
Let me, lassie, quickly die,
Still trusting that thou lo'es me –
Lassie, let me quickly die,
Still trusting that thou lo'es me!

Winter: A Dirge

THE wintry west extends his blast,
And hail and rain does blaw;
Or the stormy north sends driving forth
The blinding sleet and snaw:
While, tumbling brown, the bum comes down,
And roars frae bank to brae:
And bird and beast in covert rest,
And pass the heartless day.

"The sweeping blast, the sky o'ercast,"
The joyless winter-day
Let others fear, to me more dear
Than all the pride of May:
The tempest's howl, it soothes my soul,
My griefs it seems to join;
The leafless trees my fancy please,
Their fate resembles mine!

Thou Pow'r Supreme, whose mighty scheme
These woes of mine fulfil,
Here, firm, I rest they must be best,
Because they are thy will!
Then all I want (O do thou grant
This one request of mine)
Since to enjoy Thou dost deny,
Assist me to resign.

The Winter It Is Past – A Fragment

THE winter it is past, and the summer comes at last
    And the small birds, they sing on ev'ry tree;
Now ev'ry thing is glad, while I am very sad,
    Since my true love is parted from me.

The rose upon the breer, by the waters running clear,
    May have charms for the linnet or the bee;
Their little loves are blest, and their little hearts at rest,
    But my true love is parted from me.

A Winter Night

Poor naked wretches, wheresoe'er you are,
That bide the pelting of this pitiless storm!
How shall your houseless heads, and unfed sides,
Your loop'd and window'd raggedness, defend you
From seasons such as these?

SHAKESPEARE.

WHEN biting Boreas, fell and doure,
Sharp shivers thro' the leafless bow'r;
When Phoebus gies a short-liv'd glow'r,
    Far south the lift,
Dim-dark'ning thro' the flaky show'r,
    Or whirling drift:

Ae night the storm the steeples rocked,
Poor Labour sweet in sleep was locked,
While burns, wi' snawy wreaths up-choked,
    Wild-eddying swirl;
Or, thro' the mining outlet bocked,
    Down headlong hurl.

List'ning the doors an' winnocks rattle,
I thought me on the ourie cattle,
Or silly sheep, wha bide this brattle
    O' winter war,
And thro' the drift, deep-lairing, sprattle,
    Beneath a scar.

Ilk happing bird,-wee, helpless thing!
That, in the merry months o' spring,
Delighted me to hear thee sing,
    What comes o' thee?
Whare wilt thou cow'r thy chittering wing,
    An' close thy e'e?

Ev'n you, on murd'ring errands toil'd,
Lone from your savage homes exil'd,
The blood-stain'd roost, and sheep-cote spoil'd
    My heart forgets,
While pityless the tempest wild
    Sore on you beats.

Now Phoebe in her midnight reign,
Dark muff'd, view'd the dreary plain;
Still crowding thoughts, a pensive train,
    Rose in my soul,
When on my ear this plantive strain,
    Slow, solemn, stole –

    "Blow, blow, ye winds, with heavier gust!
    "And freeze, thou bitter-biting frost!
    "Descend, ye chilly, smothering snows!
    "Not all your rage, as now, united shows
    "More hard unkindness unrelenting,
    "Vengeful malice unrepenting.
"Than heaven-illumin'd man on brother man bestows!
    "See stern Oppression's iron grip,
    "Or mad Ambition's gory hand,
"Sending, like blood-hounds from the slip,
    "Woe, Want, and murder o'er a land!
    "Ev'n in the peaceful rural vale,
    "Truth, weeping, tells the mournful tale,
"How pamper'd Luxury, Flatt'ry by her side,
    "The parasite empoisoning her ear,
    "With all the servile wretches in the rear,
"Looks o'er proud property, extended wide;
    "And eyes the simple, rustic hind,
    "Whose toil upholds the glitt'ring show,
    "A creature of another kind,
    "Some coarser substance, unrefin'd,
"Plac'd for her lordly use thus far, thus vile, below.

"Where, where is Love's fond, tender throe,
"With lordly Honour's lofty brow,
"The pow'rs you proudly own?
"Is there, beneath Love's noble name,
"Can harbour, dark, the selfish aim,
"To bless himself alone!
"Mark maiden-innocence a prey
"To love-pretending snares:
"This boasted Honour turns away,
"Shunning soft Pity's rising sway,
"Regardless of the tears and unavailing pray'rs!
"Perhaps this hour, in mis'ry's squalid nest,
"She strains your infant to her joyless breast,
"And with a mother's fears shrinks at the rocking blast!

"Oh ye! who, sunk in beds of down,
"Feel not a want but what yourselves create,
"Think, for a moment, on his wretched fate,
"Whom friends and fortune quite disown!
"Ill-satisfied keen nature's clam'rous call,
"Stretch'd on his straw, he lays himself to sleep;
"While thro' the ragged roof and chinky wall,
"Chill, o'er his slumbers, piles the drifty heap!
"Think on the dungeon's grim confine,
"Where Guilt and poor misfortune pine!
"Guilt, erring man, relenting view!
"But shall thy legal rage pursue
"The wretch, already crushed low,
"By cruel Fortune's undeserved blow?
"Affliction's sons are brothers in distress;
"A brother to relieve, how exquisite the bliss!"

I heard nae mair, for Chanticleer
    Shook off the pouthery snaw,
And hail'd the morning with a cheer,
    A cottage-rousing craw.

But deep this truth impress'd my mind
    Thro' all His works abroad,
The heart benevolent and kind
    The most resembles God.

The Winter Of Life

BUT lately seen in gladsome green,
    The woods rejoic'd the day,
Thro' gentle showers, the laughing flowers
    In double pride were gay:
But now our joys are fled
    On winter blasts awa!
Yet maiden May, in rich array,
    Again shall bring them a'.

But my white pow, nae kindly thowe
    Shall melt the snaws of age;
My trunk of eild, but buss or beild,
    Sinks in time's wintry rage.
Oh, age has weary days,
    And nights o' sleepless pain:
Thou golden time, o' youthfu' prime,
    Why comes thou not again?

Ye Flowery Banks

Ye flowery banks o' bonie Doon,
    How can ye blume sae fair!
How can ye chant, ye little birds,
    And I sae fu' o' care?

Thou'll break my heart, thou bonie bird,
    That sings upon the bough;
Thou minds me o' the happy days,
    When my fause luve was true.

Thou'll break my heart, thou bonie bird,
    That sings beside thy mate;
For sae I sat, and sae I sang,
    And wist na o' my fate.

Aft hae I rov'd by bonie Doon
    To see the wood-bine twine,
And ilka bird sang o' its luve,
    And sae did I o' mine.

Wi' lightsome heart I pu'd a rose
    Frae aff its thorny tree;
And my fause luver staw my rose
    But left the thorn wi' me.

Glossary

A
A', all.
A-back, behind, away.
Abiegh, aloof, off.
Ablins, v. aiblins.
Aboon, above up.
Abread, abroad.
Abreed, in breadth.
Ae, one.
Aff, off.
Aff-hand, at once.
Aff-loof, offhand.
A-fiel, afield.
Afore, before.
Aft, oft.
Aften, often.
Agley, awry.
Ahin, behind.
Aiblins, perhaps.
Aidle, foul water.
Aik, oak.
Aiken, oaken.
Ain, own.
Air, early.
Airle, earnest money.
Airn, iron.
Airt, direction.
Airt, to direct.
Aith, oath.
Aits, oats.
Aiver, an old horse.
Aizle, a cinder.
A-jee, ajar; to one side.
Alake, alas.
Alane, alone.
Alang, along.
Amaist, almost.
Amang, among.

An, if.
An', and.
Ance, once.
Ane, one.
Aneath, beneath.
Anes, ones.
Anither, another.
Aqua-fontis, spring water.
Aqua-vitae, whiskey.
Arle, v. airle.
Ase, ashes.
Asklent, askew, askance.
Aspar, aspread.
Asteer, astir.
A'thegither, altogether.
Athort, athwart.
Atweel, in truth.
Atween, between.
Aught, eight.
Aught, possessed of.
Aughten, eighteen.
Aughtlins, at all.
Auld, old.
Auldfarran, auldfarrant,
   shrewd, old-fashioned,
      sagacious.
Auld Reekie, Edinburgh.
Auld-warld, old-world.
Aumous, alms.
Ava, at all.
Awa, away.
Awald, backways and
      doubled up.
Awauk, awake.
Awauken, awaken.
Awe, owe.
Awkart, awkward.
Awnie, bearded.

Ayont, beyond.

B
Ba', a ball.
Backet, bucket, box.
Backit, backed.
Backlins-comin, coming back.
Back-yett, gate at the back.
Bade, endured.
Bade, asked.
Baggie, stomach.
Baig'nets, bayonets.
Baillie, magistrate of a Scots
    burgh.
Bainie, bony.
Bairn, child.
Bairntime, brood.
Baith, both.
Bakes, biscuits.
Ballats, ballads.
Balou, lullaby.
Ban, swear.
Ban', band (of the Presbyterian
    clergyman).
Bane, bone.
Bang, an effort; a blow; a large
    number.
Bang, to thump.
Banie, v. bainie.
Bannet, bonnet.
Bannock, bonnock, a thick
    oatmeal cake.
Bardie, dim. of bard.
Barefit, barefooted.
Barket, barked.
Barley-brie, or bree, barley-
    brew-ale or whiskey.
Barm, yeast.
Barmie, yeasty.
Barn-yard, stackyard.
Bartie, the Devil.

Bashing, abashing.
Batch, a number.
Batts, the botts; the colic.
Bauckie-bird, the bat.
Baudrons, Baudrans, the cat.
Bauk, cross-beam.
Bauk, v. bawk.
Bauk-en', beam-end.
Bauld, bold.
Bauldest, boldest.
Bauldly, boldly.
Baumy, balmy.
Bawbee, a half-penny.
Bawdrons, v. baudrons.
Bawk, a field path.
Baws'nt, white-streaked.
Bear, barley.
Beas', beasts, vermin.
Beastie, dim. of beast.
Beck, a curtsy.
Beet, feed, kindle.
Beild, v. biel.
Belang, belong.
Beld, bald.
Bellum, assault.
Bellys, bellows.
Belyve, by and by.
Ben, a parlor (i.e., the inner
    apartment); into the parlor.
Benmost, inmost.
Be-north, to the northward of.
Be-south, to the southward of.
Bethankit, grace after meat.
Beuk, a book: devil's pictur'd
    beuks-playing-cards.
Bicker, a wooden cup.
Bicker, a short run.
Bicker, to flow swiftly and with
    a slight noise.
Bickerin, noisy contention.
Bickering, hurrying.

Bid, to ask, to wish, to offer.
Bide, abide, endure.
Biel, bield, a shelter; a sheltered
    spot.
Biel, comfortable.
Bien, comfortable.
Bien, bienly, comfortably.
Big, to build.
Biggin, building.
Bike, v. byke.
Bill, the bull.
Billie, fellow, comrade, brother.
Bings, heaps.
Birdie, dim. of bird; also
    maidens.
Birk, the birch.
Birken, birchen.
Birkie, a fellow.
Birr, force, vigor.
Birring, whirring.
Birses, bristles.
Birth, berth.
Bit, small (e.g., bit lassie).
Bit, nick of time.
Bitch-fou, completely drunk.
Bizz, a flurry.
Bizz, buzz.
Bizzard, the buzzard.
Bizzie, busy.
Black-bonnet, the Presbyterian
    elder.
Black-nebbit, black-beaked.
Blad, v. blaud.
Blae, blue, livid.
Blastet, blastit, blasted.
Blastie, a blasted (i.e., damned)
    creature; a little wretch.
Blate, modest, bashful.
Blather, bladder.
Blaud, a large quantity.
Blaud, to slap, pelt.

Blaw, blow.
Blaw, to brag.
Blawing, blowing.
Blawn, blown.
Bleer, to blear.
Bleer't, bleared.
Bleeze, blaze.
Blellum, a babbler; a railer; a
blusterer.
Blether, blethers, nonsense.
Blether, to talk nonsense.
Bletherin', talking nonsense.
Blin', blind.
Blink, a glance, a moment.
Blink, to glance, to shine.
Blinkers, spies, oglers.
Blinkin, smirking, leering.
Blin't, blinded.
Blitter, the snipe.
Blue-gown, the livery of the
    licensed beggar.
Bluid, blood.
Bluidy, bloody.
Blume, to bloom.
Bluntie, a stupid.
Blypes, shreds.
Bobbed, curtsied.
Bocked, vomited.
Boddle, a farthing.
Bode, look for.
Bodkin, tailor's needle.
Body, bodie, a person.
Boggie, dim. of bog.
Bogle, a bogie, a hobgoblin.
Bole, a hole, or small recess in
    the wall.
Bonie, bonnie, pretty, beautiful.
Bonilie, prettily.
Bonnock, v. Bannock.
'Boon, above.
Boord, board, surface.

Boord-en', board-end.
Boortress, elders.
Boost, must needs.
Boot, payment to the bargain.
Bore, a chink, recess.
Botch, an angry tumor.
Bouk, a human trunk; bulk.
Bountith, bounty.
'Bout, about.
Bow-hough'd, bandy-thighed.
Bow-kail, cabbage.
Bow't, bent.
Brachens, ferns.
Brae, the slope of a hill.
Braid, broad.
Broad-claith, broad-cloth.
Braik, a harrow.
Braing't, plunged.
Brak, broke.
Brak's, broke his.
Brankie, gay, fine.
Branks, a wooden curb, a
    bridle.
Bran'y, brandy.
Brash, short attack.
Brats, small pieces, rags.
Brats, small children.
Brattle, a scamper.
Brattle, noisy onset.
Braw, handsome, fine, gaily
    dressed.
Brawlie, finely, perfectly,
    heartily.
Braxies, sheep that have died of
    braxie (a disease).
Breastie, dim. of breast.
Breastit, sprang forward.
Brechan, ferns.
Breeks, breeches.
Breer, brier.
Brent, brand.

Brent, straight, steep (i.e., not
    sloping from baldness).
Brie, v. barley-brie.
Brief, writ.
Brier, briar.
Brig, bridge.
Brisket, breast.
Brither, brother.
Brock, a badger.
Brogue, a trick.
Broo, soup, broth, water; liquid
    in which anything is
    cooked.
Brooses, wedding races from
    the church to the home of
    the bride.
Brose, a thick mixture of meal
    and warm water; also a
    synonym for porridge.
Browster wives, ale wives.
Brugh, a burgh.
Brulzie, brulyie, a brawl.
Brunstane, brimstone.
Brunt, burned.
Brust, burst.
Buckie, dim. of buck; a smart
    younker.
Buckle, a curl.
Buckskin, Virginian: the
    buckskin kye, negroes.
Budget, tinker's bag of tools.
Buff, to bang, to thump.
Bughtin, folding.
Buirdly, stalwart.
Bum, the buttocks.
Bum, to hum.
Bum-clock, beetle, cockchafer,
    Junebug.
Bummle, a drone, a useless
    fellow.
Bunker, a seat.

Bunters, harlots.
Burdies, dim. of bird or burd
    (a lady); maidens.
Bure, bore.
Burn, a rivulet.
Burnewin, the blacksmith (i.e.,
    burn the wind).
Burnie, dim. of burn, a rivulet.
Burr-thistle, spear-thistle.
Busk, to dress; to garb; to dress
    up; to adorn.
Buss, a bush.
Bussle, bustle.
But, without.
But, butt, in the kitchen (i.e.,
    the outer apartment).
By, past, aside.
By, beside.
By himsel, beside himself.
Bye attour (i.e., by and attour),
    beside and at a distance.
Byke, a bees' nest; a hive; a
    swarm; a crowd.
Byre, a cow-house.

C
Ca', call, knock, drive.
Cadger, a hawker (especially of
    fish).
Cadie, caddie, a fellow.
Caff, chaff.
Caird, a tinker.
Calf-ward, grazing plot for
    calves (i.e., churchyard).
Callan, callant, a stripling.
Caller, cool, refreshing.
Callet, a trull.
Cam, came.
Canie, cannie, gentle, tractable,
    quiet, prudent, careful.
Cankrie, crabbed.

Canna, can not.
Canniest, quietest.
Cannilie, cannily, quietly,
    prudently, cautiously.
Cantie, cheerful, lively, jolly,
    merry.
Cantraip, magic, witching.
Cants, merry stories, canters or
    sprees or merry doings.
Cape-stanc, copestone.
Capon-castrate.
Care na by, do not care.
Carl, carle, a man, an old man.
Carl-hemp, male-hemp.
Carlie, a manikin.
Carlin, carline a middle-aged,
    or old, woman; a beldam, a
    witch.
Carmagnole, a violent Jacobin.
Cartes, playing-cards.
Cartie, dim. of cart.
Catch-the-plack, the hunt for
    money.
Caudron, a caldron.
Cauf, calf.
Cauf-leather, calf-leather.
Cauk, chalk.
Cauld, cold.
Cauldron, caldron.
Caup, a wooden drinking
    vessel.
Causey-cleaners, causeway-
    cleaners.
Cavie, a hen-coop.
Chamer, chaumer, chamber.
Change-house, tavern.
Chanter, bagpipes; the pipe of
    the bag-pipes which
    produces the melody; song.
Chap, a fellow, a young fellow.
Chap, to strike.

Chapman, a pedler.
Chaup, chap, a stroke, a blow.
Chear, cheer.
Chearfu', cheerful.
Chearless, cheerless.
Cheary, cheery.
Cheek-for-chow, cheek-by-
    jowl (i.e. close beside).
Cheep, peep, squeak.
Chiel, chield (i. e., child), a
    fellow, a young fellow.
Chimla, chimney.
Chittering, shivering.
Chows, chews.
Chuck, a hen, a dear.
Chuckie, dim. of chuck, but
    usually signifies mother
    hen, an old dear.
Chuffie, fat-faced.
Chuse, to choose.
Cit, the civet.
Cit, a citizen, a merchant.
Clachan, a small village about a
    church.
Claeding, clothing.
Claes, claise, clothes.
Claith, cloth.
Claithing, clothing.
Clankie, a severe knock.
Clap, the clapper of a mill.
Clark, a clerk.
Clark, clerkly, scholarly.
Clarkit, clerked, wrote.
Clarty, dirty.
Clash, an idle tale; gossip.
Clash, to tattle.
Clatter, noise, tattle, talk,
    disputation, babble.
Clatter, to make a noise by
    striking; to babble; to
    prattle.

Claught, clutched, seized.
Claughtin, clutching, grasping.
Claut, a clutch, a handful.
Claut, to scrape.
Claver, clover.
Clavers, gossip, nonsense.
Claw, a scratch, a blow.
Claw, to scratch, to strike.
Clay-cauld, clay-cold.
Claymore, a two-handed
    Highland sword.
Cleckin, a brood.
Cleed, to clothe.
Cleek, to snatch.
Cleekit, linked arms.
Cleg, gadfly.
Clink, a sharp stroke; jingle.
Clink, money, coin.
Clink, to chink.
Clink, to rhyme.
Clinkin, with a smart motion.
Clinkum, clinkumbell, the
    beadle, the bellman.
Clips, shears.
Clish-ma-claver, gossip,
    taletelling; non-sense.
Clockin-time, clucking-
    (i. e., hatching-) time.
Cloot, the hoof.
Clootie, cloots, hoofie, hoofs
    (a nickname of the Devil).
Clour, a bump or swelling after
    a blow.
Clout, a cloth, a patch.
Clout, to patch.
Clud, a cloud.
Clunk, to make a hollow
    sound.
Coble, a broad and flat boat.
Cock, the mark (in curling).
Cockie, dim. of cock (applied

to an old man).

Cocks, fellows, good fellows.

Cod, a pillow.

Coft, bought.

Cog, a wooden drinking vessel, a porridge dish, a corn measure for horses.

Coggie, dim. of cog, a little dish.

Coil, Coila, Kyle (one of the ancient districts of Ayrshire).

Collieshangie, a squabble.

Cood, cud.

Coof, v. cuif.

Cookit, hid.

Coor, cover.

Cooser, a courser, a stallion.

Coost (i. e., cast), looped, threw off, tossed, chucked.

Cootie, a small pail.

Cootie, leg-plumed.

Corbies, ravens, crows.

Core, corps.

Corn mou, corn heap.

Corn't, fed with corn.

Corse, corpse.

Corss, cross.

Cou'dna, couldna, couldn't.

Countra, country.

Coup, to capsize.

Couthie, couthy, loving, affable, cosy, comfortable.

Cowe, to scare, to daunt.

Cowe, to lop.

Crack, tale; a chat; talk.

Crack, to chat, to talk.

Craft, croft.

Craft-rig, croft-ridge.

Craig, the throat.

Craig, a crag.

Craigie, dim. of craig, the throat.

Craigy, craggy.

Craik, the corn-crake, the land-rail.

Crambo-clink, rhyme.

Crambo-jingle, rhyming.

Cran, the support for a pot or kettle.

Crankous, fretful.

Cranks, creakings.

Cranreuch, hoar-frost.

Crap, crop, top.

Craw, crow.

Creel, an osier basket.

Creepie-chair, stool of repentance.

Creeshie, greasy.

Crocks, old ewes.

Cronie, intimate friend.

Crooded, cooed.

Croods, coos.

Croon, moan, low.

Croon, to toll.

Crooning, humming.

Croose, crouse, cocksure, set, proud, cheerful.

Crouchie, hunchbacked.

Crousely, confidently.

Crowdie, meal and cold water, meal and milk, porridge.

Crowdie-time, porridge-time (i. e., breakfast-time).

Crowlin, crawling.

Crummie, a horned cow.

Crummock, cummock, a cudgel, a crooked staff.

Crump, crisp.

Crunt, a blow.

Cuddle, to fondle.

Cuif, coof, a dolt, a ninny;

a dastard.

Cummock, v. crummock.

Curch, a kerchief for the head.
Curchie, a curtsy.

Curler, one who plays at
curling.

Curmurring, commotion.

Curpin, the crupper of a horse.

Curple, the crupper (i. e.,
buttocks).

Cushat, the wood pigeon.

Custock, the pith of the
colewort.

Cutes, feet, ankles.

Cutty, short.

Cutty-stools, stools of
repentance.

D

Dad, daddie, father.

Daez't, dazed.

Daffin, larking, fun.

Daft, mad, foolish.

Dails, planks.

Daimen icker, an odd ear of
corn.

Dam, pent-up water, urine.

Damie, dim. of dame.

Dang, pret. of ding.

Danton, v. daunton.

Darena, dare not.

Darg, labor, task, a day's work.

Darklins, in the dark.

Daud, a large piece.

Daud, to pelt.

Daunder, saunter.

Daunton, to daunt.

Daur, dare.

Daurna, dare not.

Daur't, dared.

Daut, dawte, to fondle.

Daviely, spiritless.

Daw, to dawn.

Dawds, lumps.

Dawtingly, prettily, caressingly.

Dead, death.

Dead-sweer, extremely
reluctant.

Deave, to deafen.

Deil, devil.

Deil-haet, nothing (Devil
have it).

Deil-ma-care, Devil may care.

Deleeret, delirious, mad.

Delvin, digging.

Dern'd, hid.

Descrive, to describe.

Deuk, duck.

Devel, a stunning blow.

Diddle, to move quickly.

Dight, to wipe.

Dight, winnowed, sifted.

Din, dun, muddy of
complexion.

Ding, to beat, to surpass.

Dink, trim.

Dinna, do not.

Dirl, to vibrate, to ring.

Diz'n, dizzen, dozen.

Dochter, daughter.

Doited, muddled, doting;
stupid, bewildered.

Donsie, vicious, bad-tempered;
restive; testy.

Dool, wo, sorrow.

Doolfu', doleful, woful.

Dorty, pettish.

Douce, douse, sedate, sober,
prudent.

Douce, doucely, dousely,
sedately, prudently.

Doudl'd, dandled.

Dought (pret. of dow), could.

Douked, ducked.

Doup, the bottom.

Doup-skelper, bottom-smacker.

Dour-doure, stubborn, obstinate; cutting.

Dow, dowe, am (is or are) able, can.

Dow, a dove.

Dowf, dowff, dull.

Dowie, drooping, mournful.

Dowilie, drooping.

Downa, can not.

Downa-do (can not do), lack of power.

Doylt, stupid, stupefied.

Doytin, doddering.,

Dozen'd, torpid.

Dozin, torpid.

Draigl't, draggled.

Drant, prosing.

Drap, drop.

Draunting, tedious.

Dree, endure, suffer.

Dreigh, v. dreight.

Dribble, drizzle.

Driddle, to toddle.

Dreigh, tedious, dull.

Droddum, the breech.

Drone, part of the bagpipe.

Droop-rumpl't, short-rumped.

Drouk, to wet, to drench.

Droukit, wetted.

Drouth, thirst.

Drouthy, thirsty.

Druken, drucken, drunken.

Drumlie, muddy, turbid.

Drummock, raw meal and cold water.

Drunt, the huff.

Dry, thirsty.

Dub, puddle, slush.

Duddie, ragged.

Duddies, dim. of duds, rags.

Duds, rags, clothes.

Dung, v. dang.

Dunted, throbbed, beat.

Dunts, blows.

Durk, dirk.

Dusht, pushed or thrown down violently.

Dwalling, dwelling.

Dwalt, dwelt.

Dyke, a fence (of stone or turf), a wall.

Dyvor, a bankrupt.

E

Ear', early.

Earn, eagle.

Eastlin, eastern.

E'e, eye.

E'ebrie, eyebrow.

Een, eyes.

E'en, even.

E'en, evening.

E'enin', evening.

E'er, ever.

Eerie, apprehensive; inspiring ghostly fear.

Eild, eld.

Eke, also.

Elbuck, elbow.

Eldritch, unearthly, haunted, fearsome.

Elekit, elected.

Ell (Scots), thirty-seven inches.

Eller, elder.

En', end.

Eneugh, enough.

Enfauld, infold.

Enow, enough.

Erse, Gaelic.
Ether-stane, adder-stone.
Ettle, aim.
Evermair, evermore.
Ev'n down, downright, positive.
Eydent, diligent.

F
Fa', fall.
Fa', lot, portion.
Fa', to get; suit; claim.
Faddom'd, fathomed.
Fae, foe.
Faem, foam.
Faiket, let off, excused.
Fain, fond, glad.
Fainness, fondness.
Fair fa', good befall! welcome.
Fairin., a present from a fair.
Fallow, fellow.
Fa'n, fallen.
Fand, found.
Far-aff, far-off.
Farls, oat-cakes.
Fash, annoyance.
Fash, to trouble; worry.
Fash'd, fash't, bothered; irked.
Fashious, troublesome.
Fasten-e'en, Fasten's Even (the evening before Lent).
Faught, a fight.
Fauld, the sheep-fold.
Fauld, folded.
Faulding, sheep-folding.
Faun, fallen.
Fause, false.
Fause-house, hole in a cornstack.
Faut, fault.
Fautor, transgressor.

Fawsont, seemly, well-doing; good-looking.
Feat, spruce.
Fecht, fight.
Feck, the bulk, the most part.
Feck, value, return.
Fecket, waistcoat; sleeve waistcoat (used by farm-servants as both vest and jacket).
Feckless, weak, pithless, feeble.
Feckly, mostly.
Feg, a fig.
Fegs, faith
Feide, feud.
Feint, v. fient.
Feirrie, lusty.
Fell, keen, cruel, dreadful, deadly; pungent.
Fell, the cuticle under the skin.
Felly, relentless.
Fen', a shift.
Fen', fend, to look after; to care for; keep off.
Fenceless, defenseless.
Ferlie, ferly, a wonder.
Ferlie, to marvel.
Fetches, catches, gurgles.
Fetch't, stopped suddenly.
Fey, fated to death.
Fidge, to fidget, to wriggle.
Fidgin-fain, tingling-wild.
Fiel, well.
Fient, fiend, a petty oath.
Fient a, not a, devil a.
Fient haet, nothing (fiend have it).
Fient haet o', not one of.
Fient-ma-care, the fiend may care (I don't!).
Fier, fiere, companion.

Fier, sound, active.
Fin', to find.
Fissle, tingle, fidget with
    delight.
Fit, foot.
Fittie-lan', the near horse of
    the hind-most pair in the
    plough.
Flae, a flea.
Flaffin, flapping.
Flainin, flannen, flannel.
Flang, flung.
Flee, to fly.
Fleech, wheedle.
Fleesh, fleece.
Fleg, scare, blow, jerk.
Fleth'rin, flattering.
Flewit, a sharp lash.
Fley, to scare.
Flichterin, fluttering.
Flinders, shreds, broken pieces.
Flinging, kicking out in
    dancing; capering.
Flingin-tree, a piece of timber
    hung by way of partition
    between two horses in a
    stable; a flail.
Fliskit, fretted, capered.
Flit, to shift.
Flittering, fluttering.
Flyte, scold.
Fock, focks, folk.
Fodgel, dumpy.
Foor, fared (i. e., went).
Foorsday, Thursday.
Forbears, forebears, forefathers.
Forby, forbye, besides.
Forfairn, worn out; forlorn.
Forfoughten, exhausted.
Forgather, to meet with.
Forgie, to forgive.

Forjesket, jaded.
Forrit, forward.
Fother, fodder.
Fou, fow, full (i. e., drunk).
Foughten, troubled.
Foumart, a polecat.
Foursome, a quartet.
Fouth, fulness, abundance.
Fow, v. fou.
Fow, a bushel.
Frae, from.
Freath, to froth,
Fremit, estranged, hostile.
Fu', full.
Fu'-han't, full-handed.
Fud, a short tail (of a rabbit or
    hare).
Fuff't, puffed.
Fur, furr, a furrow.
Fur-ahin, the hindmost
    plough-horse in the
    furrow.
Furder, success.
Furder, to succeed.
Furm, a wooden form.
Fusionless, pithless, sapless,
    tasteless,
Fyke, fret.
Fyke, to fuss; fidget.
Fyle, to defile, to foul.

G
Gab, the mouth.
Gab, to talk.
Gabs, talk.
Gae, gave.
Gae, to go.
Gaed, went.
Gaen, gone.
Gaets, ways, manners.
Gairs, gores.

Gane, gone.
Gang, to go.
Gangrel, vagrant.
Gar, to cause, to make, to
    compel.
Garcock, the moorcock.
Garten, garter.
Gash, wise; self-complacent
    (implying prudence and
    prosperity); talkative.
Gashing, talking, gabbing.
Gat, got.
Gate, way-road, manner.
Gatty, enervated.
Gaucie, v. Gawsie.
Gaud, a. goad.
Gaudsman, goadsman, driver of
    the plough-team.
Gau'n. gavin.
Gaun, going.
Gaunted, gaped, yawned.
Gawky, a foolish woman or lad.
Gawky, foolish.
Gawsie, buxom; jolly.
Gaylies, gaily, rather.
Gear, money, wealth; goods;
    stuff.
Geck, to sport; toss the head.
Ged. a pike.
Gentles, gentry.
Genty, trim and elegant.
Geordie, dim. of George, a
    guinea.
Get, issue, offspring, breed.
Ghaist, ghost.
Gie, to give.
Gied, gave.
Gien, given.
Gif, if.
Giftie, dim. of gift.

Giglets, giggling youngsters or
    maids.
Gillie, dim. of gill (glass of
    whiskey).
Gilpey, young girl.
Gimmer, a young ewe.
Gin, if, should, whether; by.
Girdle, plate of metal for firing
    cakes, bannocks.
Girn, to grin, to twist the face
    (but from pain or rage, not
    joy); gapes; snarls.
Gizz, wig.
Glaikit, foolish, thoughtless,
    giddy.
Glaizie, glossy, shiny.
Glaum'd, grasped.
Gled, a hawk, a kite.
Gleede, a glowing coal.
Gleg, nimble, sharp, keen-
    witted.
Gleg, smartly.
Glieb, a portion of land.
Glib-gabbet, smooth-tongued.
Glint, sparkle.
Gloamin, twilight; gloamin-
    shot, sunset.
Glow'r, stare.
Glunch, frown, growl.
Goavin, looking dazedlyl;
    mooning.
Gotten, got.
Gowan, the wild, or mountain,
    daisy.
Gowany, covered with wild
    daisies.
Gowd, gold.
Gowdie, the head.
Gowff'd, struck, as in the game
    of golf.

Gowk, the cuckoo, a dolt.

Gowling, lamenting (as a dog in grief).

Graff, a grave, a vault.

Grain'd, groaned.

Graip, a dung-fork.

Graith, implements, gear; furniture; attire.

Graithing, gearing, vestments.

Grane, groan.

Grannie, graunie, grandmother.

Grape, grope.

Grat, wept.

Gree, the prize (degree).

Gree, to agree.

Greet, to weep.

Groanin maut, groaning malt, brewed for a lying-in.

Grozet, a gooseberry.

Grumphie, the pig.

Grun', the ground.

Gruntle, the face.

Gruntle, dim. of grunt.

Grunzie, growing.

Grutten, wept.

Gude, God.

Guid, gude, good.

Guid-e'en, good evening.

Guid-father, father-in-law.

Guid-man, husband.

Guid-wife. mistress of the house.

Guid-willie, hearty, full of good-will.

Gullie, gully, a large knife.

Gulravage, riotous play.

Gumlie, muddy.

Gumption, wisdom.

Gusty, tasty.

Gutcher, goodsire, grandfather.

H

Ha', hall.

Ha' folk, the servants.

Haddin, holding, inheritance.

Hae, have.

Haet, a thing.

Haffet, hauffet, the temple, the side of the head.

Haffets, side-locks.

Hafflins, half, partly.

Hag, a moss, a broken bog.

Haggis, a special Scots pudding, made of sheep's lungs, liver and heart, onions and oatmeal, boiled in a sheep's stomach.

Hain, to spare, to save.

Hairst, har'st, harvest.

Haith, faith (an oath).

Haivers, v. havers.

Hal', hald, holding, possession.

Hale, hail, the whole.

Hale, health.

Hale, hail, whole, healthy.

Halesome, wholesome.

Hallan, a partition wall, a porch, outer door.

Halloween, All Saints' Eve (31st of October).

Hallowmas, All Saints' Day (1st of November).

Haly, holy.

Hame, home,

Han', haun, hand.

Han-darg, v. darg.

Hand-wal'd, hand-picked (i.e., choicest).

Hangie, hangman (nickname of the Devil).

Hansel, the first gift; earnest.

Hap, a wrap, a covering against cold.
Hap, to shelter.
Hap, to hop.
Happer, hopper (of a mill).
Hap-step-an'-lowp. hop-step-and-jump.
Harkit, hearkened.
Harn, coarse cloth.
Hash, an oaf.
Haslock woo, the wool on the neck of a sheep.
Haud, to hold, to keep.
Hauf, half.
Haughs, low-lying rich lands by a river.
Haun, v. han',
Haurl, to trail.
Hause, cuddle, embrace.
Haveril, hav'rel, one who talks nonsense.
Havers, nonsense.
Havins, manners, conduct.
Hawkie, a white-faced cow; a cow.
Heal, v. hale.
Healsome, v. halesome.
Hecht, to promise; threaten.
Heckle, a flax-comb.
Heels-o'er-gowdie, v. gowdie.
Heeze, to hoist.
Heich, heigh, high.
Hem-shin'd, crooked-shin'd.
Herd, a herd-boy.
Here awa, hereabout.
Herry, to harry.
Herryment, spoliation.
Hersel, herself.
Het, hot.
Heugh, a hollow or pit; a crag, a steep bank.

Heuk, a hook.
Hilch, to hobble.
Hiltie-skiltie, helter-skelter.
Himsel, himselfk
Hiney, hinny, honey.
Hing, to hang.
Hirple, to move unevenly; to limp.
Hissels, so many cattle as one person can attend (R. B.).
Histie, bare.
Hizzie, a hussy, a wench.
Hoast, cough.
Hoddin, the motion of a sage countryman riding on a cart-horse (R. B.).
Hoddin-grey, coarse gray woolen.
Hoggie, dim. of hog; a lamb.
Hog-score, a line on the curling rink.
Hog-shouther, a kind of horse-play by jostling with the shoulder; to jostle.
Hoodie-craw, the hooded crow, the carrion crow.
Hoodock, grasping, vulturish.
Hooked, caught.
Hool, the outer case, the sheath.
Hoolie, softly.
Hoord, hoard.
Hoordet, hoarded.
Horn, a horn spoon; a comb of horn.
Hornie, the Devil.
Host, v. hoast.
Hotch'd, jerked.
Houghmagandie, fornication.
Houlet, v. howlet.
Houpe, hope.

Hove, swell.

Howdie, howdy, a midwife.

Howe, hollow.

Howk, to dig.

Howlet, the owl.

Hoyse, a hoist.

Hoy't, urged (R. B.).

Hoyte, to amble crazily (R. B.).

Hughoc, dim. of Hugh.

Hullions, slovens.

Hunder, a hundred.

Hunkers, hams.

Hurcheon, the hedgehog.

Hurchin, urchin.

Hurdies, the loins, the crupper
(R. B.) (i. e., the buttocks).

Hurl, to trundle.

Hushion, a footless stocking.

Hyte, furious.

I

I', in.

Icker, an ear of corn.

Ier-oe, a great-grandchild.

Ilk, ilka, each, every.

Ill o't, bad at it.

Ill-taen, ill-taken.

Ill-thief. the Devil.

Ill-willie, ill-natured, niggardly.

Indentin, indenturing.

Ingine, genius, ingenuity; wit.

Ingle, the fire, the fireside.

Ingle-cheek, fireside (properly
the jamb of the fireplace).

Ingle-lowe, ingle-low, flame of
the fire.

I'se, I shall, or will.

Itsel', itself.

Ither, other, another.

J

Jad, a jade.

Janwar, January.

Jauk, to trifle, to dally.

Jauner, gabber.

Jauntie, dim. of jaunt.

Jaup, splash.

Jaw, talk, impudence.

Jaw, to throw, to dash.

Jeeg, to jog.

Jillet, a jilt.

Jimp, small, slender.

Jimply, neatly.

Jimps, stays.

Jink, the slip.

Jink, to frisk, to sport, to dodge.

Jinker, dodger (coquette); a
jinker noble; a noble goer.

Jirkinet, bodice.

Jirt, a jerk.

Jiz, a wig.

Jo, a sweetheart.

Jocteleg, a clasp-knife.

Jouk, to duck, to cover, to
dodge.

Jow, to jow, a verb which
included both the swinging
motion and pealing sound
of a large bell (R.B.).

Jumpet, jumpit, jumped.

Jundie, to jostle.

Jurr, a servant wench.

K

Kae, a jackdaw.

Kail, kale, the colewort;
cabbage; Scots' broth.

Kail-blade, the leaf of the
colewort.

Kail-gullie, a cabbage knife.
Kail-runt, the stem of the
    colewort.
Kail-whittle, a cabbage knife.
Kail-yard, a kitchen garden.
Kain, kane, rents in kind.
Kame, a comb.
Kebars, rafters.
Kebbuck, a cheese; a kebbuck
    heel = the last crust of a
    cheese.
Keckle, to cackle, to giggle.
Keek, look, glance.
Keekin-glass, the looking-glass.
Keel, red chalk.
Kelpies, river demons.
Ken, to know.
Kenna, know not.
Kennin, a very little (merely as
    much as can be perceived).
Kep, to catch.
Ket, the fleece on a sheep's
    body.
Key, quay.
Kiaugh, anxiety.
Kilt, to tuck up.
Kimmer, a wench, a gossip; a
    wife.
Kin', kind.
King's-hood, the 2d stomach in
    a ruminant (equivocal for
    the scrotum).
Kintra, country.
Kirk, church.
Kirn, a churn.
Kirn, harvest home.
Kirsen, to christen.
Kist, chest, counter.
Kitchen, to relish.
Kittle, difficult, ticklish, delicate,
    fickle.

Kittle, to tickle.
Kittlin, kitten.
Kiutlin, cuddling.
Knaggie, knobby.
Knappin-hammers, hammers
    for breaking stones.
Knowe, knoll.
Knurl, knurlin, dwarf.
Kye, cows.
Kytes, bellies.
Kythe, to show.

L

Laddie, dim. of lad.
Lade, a load.
Lag, backward.
Laggen, the bottom angle of a
    wooden dish.
Laigh, low.
Laik, lack.
Lair, lore, learning.
Laird, landowner.
Lairing, sticking or sinking in
    moss or mud.
Laith, loath.
Laithfu', loathful, sheepish.
Lallan, lowland.
Lallans, Scots Lowland
    vernacular.
Lammie, dim. of lamb.
Lan', land.
Lan'-afore, the foremost horse
    on the unplowed land side.
Lan'-ahin, the hindmost horse
    on the unplowed land side.
Lane, lone.
Lang, long.
Lang syne, long since, long ago.
Lap, leapt.
Lave, the rest.
Laverock, lav'rock, the lark.

Lawin, the reckoning.
Lea, grass, untilled land.
Lear, lore, learning.
Leddy, lady.
Lee-lang, live-long.
Leesome, lawful.
Leeze me on, dear is to me; blessings on; commend me.
Leister, a fish-spear.
Len', to lend.
Leugh, laugh'd.
Leuk, look.
Ley-crap, lea-crop.
Libbet, castrated.
Licks, a beating.
Lien, lain.
Lieve, lief.
Lift, the sky.
Lift, a load.
Lightly, to disparage, to scorn.
Lilt, to sing.
Limmer, to jade; mistress.
Lin, v. linn.
Linn, a waterfall.
Lint, flax.
Lint-white, flax-colored.
Lintwhite, the linnet.
Lippen'd, trusted.
Lippie, dim. of lip.
Loan, a lane,
Loanin, the private road leading to a farm.
Lo'ed, loved.
Lon'on, London.
Loof (pl. looves), the palm of the hand.
Loon, loun, lown, a fellow, a varlet.
Loosome, lovable.
Loot, let.
Loove, love.

Looves, v. loof.
Losh, a minced oath.
Lough, a pond, a lake.
Loup, lowp, to leap.
Low, lowe, a flame.
Lowin, lowing, flaming, burning.
Lown, v. loon.
Lowp, v. loup.
Lowse, louse, to untie, let loose.
Lucky, a grandmother, an old woman; an ale wife.
Lug, the ear.
Lugget, having ears.
Luggie, a porringer.
Lum, the chimney.
Lume, a loom.
Lunardi, a balloon bonnet.
Lunches, full portions.
Lunt, a column of smoke or steam.
Luntin, smoking.
Luve, love.
Lyart, gray in general; discolored by decay or old age.
Lynin, lining.

M

Mae, more.
Mailen, mailin, a farm.
Mailie, Molly.
Mair, more.
Maist. most.
Maist, almost.
Mak, make.
Mak o', make o', to pet, to fondle.
Mall, Mally.
Manteele, a mantle.
Mark, merk, an old Scots coin

(13 1–3d. sterling).
Mashlum, of mixed meal.
Maskin-pat, the teapot.
Maukin, a hare.
Maun, must.
Maunna, mustn't.
Maut, malt.
Mavis, the thrush.
Mawin, mowing.
Mawn, mown.
Mawn, a large basket.
Mear, a mare.
Meikle, mickle, muckle, much,
    great.
Melder, a grinding corn.
Mell, to meddle.
Melvie, to powder with
    meal-dust.
Men', mend.
Mense, tact, discretion,
    politeness.
Menseless, unmannerly.
Merle, the blackbird.
Merran, Marian.
Mess John, Mass John, the
    parish priest, the minister.
Messin, a cur, a mongrel.
Midden, a dunghill.
Midden-creels, manure-baskets.
Midden dub, midden puddle.
Midden-hole, a gutter at the
    bottom of the dunghill.
Milking shiel, the milking shed.
Mim, prim, affectedly meek.
Mim-mou'd, prim-lipped.
Min', mind, remembrance.
Mind, to remember, to bear in
    mind.
Minnie, mother.
Mirk, dark.
Misca', to miscall, to abuse.

Mishanter, mishap.
Mislear'd, mischievous,
    unmannerly.
Mistak, mistake.
Misteuk, mistook.
Mither, mother.
Mixtie-maxtie, confused.
Monie, many.
Mools, crumbling earth, grave.
Moop, to nibble, to keep close
    company, to meddle.
Mottie, dusty.
Mou', the mouth.
Moudieworts, moles.
Muckle, v. meikle.
Muslin-kail, beefless broth.
Mutchkin, an English pint.

N
Na, nae, no, not.
Naething, naithing, nothing.
Naig, a nag.
Nane, none,
Nappy, ale, liquor.
Natch, a notching implement;
    abuse.
Neebor, neibor, neighbor.
Needna, needn't.
Neist, next.
Neuk, newk, a nook, a corner.
New-ca'd, newly driven.
Nick (Auld), Nickie-ben, a
    name of the Devil.
Nick, to sever; to slit; to nail,
    to seize away.
Nickie-ben, v. Nick.
Nick-nackets, curiosities.
Nicks, cuts; the rings on a
    cow's horns.
Nieve, the fist.
Nieve-fu', fistful.

Niffer, exchange.
Nit, a nut.
No, not.
Nocht, nothing.
Norland, northern.
Nowt, nowte, cattle.

O
O', of.
O'erword, the refrain;
    catchword.
Onie, any.
Or, ere, before.
Orra, extra.
O't, of it.
Ought, aught.
Oughtlins, aughtlins, aught in
    the least; at all.
Ourie, shivering, drooping.
Outler, unhoused.
Owre, over, too.
Owsen, oxen.
Owthor, author.
Oxter'd, held up under the
    arms.

P
Pack an' thick, confidential.
Paidle, to paddle, to wade; to
    walk with a weak action.
Paidle, nail-bag.
Painch, the paunch.
Paitrick, a partridge; used
    equivocally of a wanton
    girl.
Pang, to cram.
Parishen, the parish.
Parritch, porridge.
Parritch-pats, porridge-pots.
Pat, pot.
Pat, put.

Pattle, pettle, a plow-staff.
Paughty, haughty.
Paukie, pauky, pawkie, artful,
    sly.
Pechan, the stomach.
Pechin, panting, blowing.
Penny-fee, wage in money.
Penny-wheep, small beer.
Pettle, v. pattle.
Philibeg, the Highlander's kilt.
Phraisin, flattering, wheedling.
Phrase, to flatter, to wheedle.
Pickle, a few, a little.
Pint (Scots), three imperial
    pints.
Pit, put.
Placads, proclamations.
Plack, four pennies (Scots).
Plackless, penniless.
Plaiden, coarse woolen cloth.
Plaister, plaster.
Plenish'd, stocked.
Pleugh, plew, a plow.
Pliskie, a trick.
Pliver, a plover.
Pock, a poke, a bag, a wallet.
Poind, to seize, to distrain, to
    impound.
Poortith, poverty.
Pou, to pull.
Pouch, pocket.
Pouk, to poke.
Poupit, pulpit.
Pouse, a push.
Poussie, a hare (also a cat).
Pouther, powther, powder.
Pouts, chicks.
Pow, the poll, the head.
Pownie, a pony.
Pow't, pulled.
Pree'd, pried (proved), tasted.

Preen, a pin.
Prent, print.
Prie, to taste.
Prief, proof.
Priggin, haggling.
Primsie, dim. of prim, precise.
Proveses, provosts.
Pu', to pull.
Puddock-stools, toadstools,
    mushrooms.
Puir, poor.
Pun', pund, pound.
Pursie, dim. of purse.
Pussie, a hare.
Pyet, a magpie.
Pyke, to pick.
Pyles, grains.

Q
Quat, quit, quitted.
Quean, a young woman, a lass.
Queir, choir.
Quey, a young cow.
Quietlin-wise, quietly.
Quo', quod, quoth.

R
Rab, rob.
Rade, rode.
Raep, a rope.
Ragweed, ragwort.
Raibles, recites by rote.
Rair, to roar.
Rairin, roaring.
Rair't, roared.
Raise, rase, rose.
Raize, to excite, anger.
Ramfeezl'd, exhausted.
Ramgunshoch, surly.
Ram-stam, headlong.
Randie, lawless, obstreperous.

Randie, randy, a scoundrel,
    a rascal.
Rant, to rollick, to roister.
Rants, merry meetings; rows.
Rape, v. raep.
Raploch, homespun.
Rash, a rush.
Rash-buss, a clump of rushes.
Rashy, rushy.
Rattan, rattoon, a rat.
Ratton-key, the rat-quay.
Raucle, rough, bitter, sturdy.
Raught, reached.
Raw, a row.
Rax, to stretch, to extend.
Ream, cream, foam.
Ream, to cream, to foam.
Reave, to rob.
Rebute, rebuff.
Red, advised, afraid.
Red, rede, to advise, to counsel.
Red-wat-shod, red-wet-shod.
Red-wud, stark mad.
Reek, smoke.
Reekie, reeky, smoky.
Reestit, scorched.
Reestit, refused to go.
Reif, theiving.
Remead, remedy.
Rickles, small stacks of corn in
    the fields.
Rief, plunder.
Rig, a ridge.
Riggin, the roof-tree, the roof.
Rigwoodie, lean.
Rin, to run.
Ripp, a handful of corn from
    the sheaf.
Ripplin-kame, the wool or flax
    comb.
Riskit, cracked.

Rive, to split, to tear, to tug, to burst.
Rock, a distaff.
Rockin, a social meeting.
Roon, round, shred.
Roose, to praise, to flatter.
Roose, reputation.
Roosty, rusty.
Rottan, a rat.
Roun', round.
Roupet, exhausted in voice.
Routh, v. rowth.
Routhie, well-stocked.
Row, rowe, to roll; to flow, as a river; to wrap.
Rowte, to low, to bellow.
Rowth, plenty, a store.
Rozet, resin.
Run-deils, downright devils.
Rung, a cudgel.
Runkl'd, wrinkled.
Runt, a cabbage or colewort stalk.
Ryke, to reach.

S
Sab, to sob.
Sae, so.
Saft, soft.
Sair, sore, hard, severe, strong.
Sair, to serve.
Sair, sairly, sorely.
Sairie, sorrowful, sorry.
Sall, shall.
Sandy, Sannack, dim. of Alexander.
Sark, a shirt.
Saugh, the willow.
Saul, soul.
Saumont, sawmont, the salmon.
Saunt, saint.

Saut, salt.
Saut-backets, v. backets.
Saw, to sow.
Sawney, v. sandy.
Sax, six.
Scar, to scare.
Scar, v. scaur.
Scathe, scaith, damage; v. skaith.
Scaud, to scald.
Scaul, scold.
Scauld, to scold.
Scaur, afraid; apt to be scared.
Scaur, a jutting rock or bank of earth.
Scho, she.
Scone, a soft flour cake.
Sconner, disgust.
Sconner, sicken.
Scraichin, calling hoarsely.
Screed, a rip, a rent.
Screed, to repeat rapidly, to rattle.
Scriechin, screeching.
Scriegh, skriegh, v. skriegh.
Scrievin, careering.
Scrimpit, scanty.
Scroggie, scroggy, scrubby.
Sculdudd'ry, bawdry.
See'd, saw.
Seisins, freehold possessions.
Sel, sel', sell, self.
Sell'd, sell't, sold.
Semple, simple.
Sen', send.
Set, to set off; to start.
Set, sat.
Sets, becomes.
Shachl'd, shapeless.
Shaird, shred, shard.
Shanagan, a cleft stick.
Shanna, shall not.

Shaul, shallow.
Shaver, a funny fellow.
Shavie, trick.
Shaw, a wood.
Shaw, to show.
Shearer, a reaper.
Sheep-shank, a sheep's trotter; nae sheep-shank bane = a person of no small importance.
Sheerly, wholly.
Sheers, scissors.
Sherra-moor, sheriffmuir.
Sheugh, a ditch, a furrow; gutter.
Sheuk, shook.
Shiel, a shed, cottage.
Shill, shrill.
Shog, a shake.
Shool, a shovel.
Shoon, shoes.
Shore, to offer, to threaten.
Short syne, a little while ago.
Shouldna, should not.
Shouther, showther, shoulder.
Shure, shore (did shear).
Sic, such.
Siccan, such a.
Sicker, steady, certain; sicker score = strict conditions.
Sidelins, sideways.
Siller, silver; money in general.
Simmer, summer.
Sin, son.
Sin', since.
Sindry, sundry.
Singet, singed, shriveled.
Sinn, the sun.
Sinny, sunny.
Skaith, damage.
Skeigh, skiegh, skittish.

Skellum, a good-for-nothing.
Skelp, a slap, a smack.
Skelp, to spank; skelpin at it = driving at it.
Skelpie-limmer's-face, a technical term in female scolding (R. B.).
Skelvy, shelvy.
Skiegh, v. skeigh.
Skinking, watery.
Skinklin, glittering.
Skirl, to cry or sound shrilly.
Sklent, a slant, a turn.
Sklent, to slant, to squint, to cheat.
Skouth, scope.
Skriech, a scream.
Skriegh, to scream, to whinny.
Skyrin, flaring.
Skyte, squirt, lash.
Slade, slid.
Slae, the sloe.
Slap, a breach in a fence; a gate.
Slaw, slow.
Slee, sly, ingenious.
Sleekit, sleek, crafty.
Slidd'ry, slippery.
Sloken, to slake.
Slypet, slipped.
Sma', small.
Smeddum, a powder.
Smeek, smoke.
Smiddy, smithy.
Smoor'd, smothered.
Smoutie, smutty.
Smytrie, a small collection; a litter.
Snakin, sneering.
Snap smart.
Snapper, to stumble.
Snash, abuse.

Snaw, snow.
Snaw-broo, snow-brew (melted
    snow).
Sned, to lop, to prune.
Sneeshin mill, a snuff-box.
Snell, bitter, biting.
Snick, a latch; snick-drawing =
    scheming; he weel a snick
    can draw = he is good at
    cheating.
Snirtle, to snigger.
Snoods, fillets worn by maids.
Snool, to cringe, to snub.
Snoove, to go slowly.
Snowkit, snuffed.
Sodger, soger, a soldier.
Sonsie, sonsy, pleasant, good-
    natured, jolly.
Soom, to swim.
Soor, sour.
Sough, v. sugh.
Souk, suck.
Soupe, sup, liquid.
Souple, supple.
Souter, cobbler.
Sowens, porridge of oat flour.
Sowps, sups.
Sowth, to hum or whistle in a
    low tune.
Sowther, to solder.
Spae, to foretell.
Spails, chips.
Spairge, to splash; to spatter.
Spak, spoke.
Spates, floods.
Spavie, the spavin.
Spavit, spavined.
Spean, to wean.
Speat, a flood.
Speel, to climb.
Speer, spier, to ask.

Speet, to spit.
Spence, the parlor.
Spier. v. speer.
Spleuchan, pouch.
Splore, a frolic; a carousal.
Sprachl'd, clambered.
Sprattle, scramble.
Spreckled, speckled.
Spring, a quick tune; a dance.
Sprittie, full of roots or sprouts
    (a kind of rush).
Sprush, spruce.
Spunk, a match; a spark; fire,
    spirit.
Spunkie, full of spirit.
Spunkie, liquor, spirits.
Spunkies, jack-o'-lanterns, will-
    o'-wisps.
Spurtle-blade, the pot-stick.
Squatter, to flap.
Squattle, to squat; to settle.
Stacher, to totter.
Staggie, dim. of staig.
Staig, a young horse.
Stan', stand.
Stane, stone.
Stan't, stood.
Stang, sting.
Stank, a moat; a pond.
Stap, to stop.
Stapple, a stopper.
Stark, strong.
Starnies, dim. of starn, star.
Starns, stars.
Startle, to course.
Staumrel, half-witted.
Staw, a stall.
Staw, to surfeit; to sicken.
Staw, stole.
Stechin, cramming.
Steek, a stitch.

Steek, to shut; to close.

Steek, to shut; to touch, meddle with.

Steeve, compact.

Stell, a still.

Sten, a leap; a spring.

Sten't, sprang.

Stented, erected; set on high.

Stents, assessments, dues.

Steyest, steepest.

Stibble, stubble.

Stibble-rig, chief reaper.

Stick-an-stowe, completely.

Stilt, limp (with the aid of stilts).

Stimpart, a quarter peck.

Stirk, a young bullock.

Stock, a plant of cabbage; colewort.

Stoited, stumbled.

Stoiter'd, staggered.

Stoor, harsh, stern.

Stoun', pang, throb.

Stoure, dust.

Stourie, dusty.

Stown, stolen.

Stownlins, by stealth.

Stoyte, to stagger.

Strae death, death in bed. (i. e., on straw).

Staik, to stroke.

Strak, struck.

Strang, strong.

Straught, straight.

Straught, to stretch.

Streekit, stretched.

Striddle, to straddle.

Stron't, lanted.

Strunt, liquor.

Strunt, to swagger.

Studdie, an anvil.

Stumpie, dim. of stump; a worn quill.

Sturt, worry, trouble.

Sturt, to fret; to vex.

Sturtin, frighted, staggered.

Styme, the faintest trace.

Sucker, sugar.

Sud, should.

Sugh, sough, sigh, moan, wail, swish.

Sumph, churl.

Sune, soon.

Suthron, southern.

Swaird, sward.

Swall'd, swelled.

Swank, limber.

Swankies, strapping fellows.

Swap, exchange.

Swapped, swopped, exchanged.

Swarf, to swoon.

Swat, sweated.

Swatch, sample.

Swats, new ale.

Sweer, v. dead-sweer.

Swirl, curl.

Swirlie, twisted, knaggy.

Swith, haste; off and away.

Swither, doubt, hesitation.

Swoom, swim.

Swoor, swore.

Sybow, a young union.

Syne, since, then.

T

Tack, possession, lease.

Tacket, shoe-nail.

Tae, to.

Tae, toe.

Tae'd, toed.

Taed, toad.

Taen, taken.

Taet, small quantity.
Tairge, to target.
Tak, take.
Tald, told.
Tane, one in contrast to other.
Tangs, tongs.
Tap, top.
Tapetless, senseless.
Tapmost, topmost.
Tappet-hen, a crested hen-shaped bottle holding three quarts of claret.
Tap-pickle, the grain at the top of the stalk.
Topsalteerie, topsy-turvy.
Targe, to examine.
Tarrow, to tarry; to be reluctant, to murmur; to weary.
Tassie, a goblet.
Tauk, talk.
Tauld, told.
Tawie, tractable.
Tawpie, a foolish woman.
Tawted, matted.
Teats, small quantities.
Teen, vexation.
Tell'd, told.
Temper-pin, a fiddle-peg; the regulating pin of the spinning-wheel.
Tent, heed.
Tent, to tend; to heed; to observe.
Tentie, watchful, careful, heedful.
Tentier, more watchful.
Tentless, careless.
Tester, an old silver coin about sixpence in value.
Teugh, tough.
Teuk, took.

Thack, thatch; thack and rape = the covering of a house, and so, home necessities.
Thae, those.
Thairm, small guts; catgut (a fiddle-string).
Theckit, thatched.
Thegither, together.
Thick, v. pack an' thick.
Thieveless, forbidding, spiteful.
Thiggin, begging.
Thir, these.
Thirl'd, thrilled.
Thole, to endure; to suffer.
Thou'se, thou shalt.
Thowe, thaw.
Thowless, lazy, useless.
Thrang, busy; thronging in crowds.
Thrang, a throng.
Thrapple, the windpipe.
Thrave, twenty-four sheaves of corn.
Thraw, a twist.
Thraw, to twist; to turn; to thwart.
Thraws, throes.
Threap, maintain, argue.
Threesome, trio.
Thretteen, thirteen.
Thretty, thirty.
Thrissle, thistle.
Thristed, thirsted.
Through, mak to through = make good.
Throu'ther (through other), pell-mell.
Thummart, polecat.
Thy lane, alone.
Tight, girt, prepared.
Till, to.

Till't, to it.
Timmer, timber, material.
Tine, to lose; to be lost.
Tinkler, tinker.
Tint, lost
Tippence, twopence.
Tip, v. toop.
Tirl, to strip.
Tirl, to knock for entrance.
Tither, the other.
Tittlin, whispering.
Tocher, dowry.
Tocher, to give a dowry.
Tocher-gude, marriage portion.
Tod, the fox.
To-fa', the fall.
Toom, empty.
Toop, tup, ram.
Toss, the toast.
Toun, town; farm steading.
Tousie, shaggy.
Tout, blast.
Tow, flax, a rope.
Towmond, towmont, a
    twelvemonth.
Towsing, rumpling (equivocal).
Toyte, to totter.
Tozie, flushed with drink.
Trams, shafts.
Transmogrify, change.
Trashtrie, small trash.
Trews, trousers.
Trig, neat, trim.
Trinklin, flowing.
Trin'le, the wheel of a barrow.
Trogger, packman.
Troggin, wares.
Troke, to barter.
Trouse, trousers.
Trowth, in truth.
Trump, a jew's harp.

Tryste, a fair; a cattle-market.
Trysted, appointed.
Trysting, meeting.
Tulyie, tulzie, a squabble;
    a tussle.
Twa, two.
Twafauld, twofold, double.
Twal, twelve; the twal = twelve
    at night.
Twalpennie worth, a penny
    worth (English money).
Twang, twinge.
Twa-three, two or three.
Tway, two.
Twin, twine, to rob; to deprive;
    bereave.
Twistle, a twist; a sprain.
Tyke, a dog.
Tyne, v. tine.
Tysday, Tuesday.

U
Ulzie, oil.
Unchancy, dangerous.
Unco, remarkably, uncom-
monly, excessively.
Unco, remarkable, uncommon,
    terrible (sarcastic).
Uncos, news, strange things,
    wonders.
Unkend, unknown.
Unsicker, uncertain.
Unskaithed, unhurt.
Usquabae, usquebae, whisky.

V
Vauntie, proud.
Vera, very.
Virls, rings.
Vittle, victual, grain, food.
Vogie, vain.

W

Wa', waw, a wall.

Wab, a web.

Wabster, a weaver.

Wad, to wager.

Wad, to wed.

Wad, would, would have.

Wad'a, would have.

Wadna, would not.

Wadset, a mortgage.

Wae, woful, sorrowful.

Wae, wo; wae's me = wo is to me.

Waesucks, alas!

Wae worth, wo befall.

Wair, v. ware.

Wale, to choose.

Wale, choice.

Walie, wawlie, choice, ample, large.

Wallop, to kick; to dangle; to gallop; to dance.

Waly fa', ill befall!

Wame, the belly.

Wamefou, bellyful.

Wan, won.

Wanchancie, dangerous.

Wanrestfu', restless.

Ware, wair, to spend; bestow.

Ware, worn.

Wark, work.

Wark-lume, tool.

Warl', warld, world.

Warlock, a wizard

Warl'y, warldly, worldly.

Warran, warrant.

Warse, worse.

Warsle, warstle, wrestle.

Wast, west.

Wastrie, waste.

Wat, wet.

Wat, wot, know.

Water-fit, water-foot (the river's mouth).

Water-kelpies, v. kelpies.

Wauble, to wobble.

Waught, a draft.

Wauk, to awake.

Wauken, to awaken.

Waukin, awake.

Waukit (with toil), horny.

Waukrife, wakeful.

Waulie, jolly.

Waur, worse.

Waur, to worst.

Waur't, worsted, beat.

Wean (wee one), a child.

Weanies, babies.

Weason, weasand.

Wecht, a measure for corn.

Wee, a little; a wee = a short space or time.

Wee things, children.

Weel, well.

Weel-faured, well-favored.

Weel-gaun, well-going.

Weel-hain'd, well-saved.

Weepers, mournings (on the steeve or hat).

Werena, were not.

We'se, we shall.

Westlin, western.

Wha, who.

Whaizle, wheeze.

Whalpet, whelped.

Wham, whom.

Whan, when.

Whang, a shive.

Whang, flog.

Whar, whare, where.

Wha's whose.

Wha's, who is.
Whase, whose.
What for, whatfore, wherefore.
Whatna, what.
What reck, what matter;
    nevertheless.
Whatt, whittled.
Whaup, the curlew.
Whaur, where.
Wheep, v. penny-wheep.
Wheep, jerk.
Whid, a fib.
Whiddin, scudding.
Whids, gambols.
Whigmeleeries, crotches.
Whingin, whining.
Whins, furze.
Whirlygigums, flourishes.
Whist, silence.
Whissle, whistle.
Whitter, a draft.
Whittle, a knife.
Wi', with.
Wick a bore, hit a curling-
    stone obliquely and send it
    through an opening.
Wi's, with his.
Wi't, with it.
Widdifu', gallows-worthy.
Widdle, wriggle.
Wiel, eddy.
Wight, strong, stout.
Wighter, more influential.
Willcat wildcat.
Willyart, disordered.
Wimple, to meander.
Win, won.
Winn, to winnow.
Winna, will not.
Winnin, winding.
Winnock, window.

Winnock-bunker, v. bunker.
Win't, did wind.
Wintle, a somersault.
Wintle, to stagger; to swing; to
    wriggle.
Winze, a curse.
Wiss, wish.
Won, to dwell.
Wonner, a wonder.
Woo', wool.
Woodie, woody, a rope
    (originally of withes);
    a gallows rope.
Woodies, twigs, withes.
Wooer-babs, love-knots.
Wordy, worthy.
Worset, worsted.
Worth, v. wae worth.
Wraith, ghost.
Wrang, wrong.
Wud, wild, mad.
Wumble, wimble.
Wyliecoat, undervest.
Wyte (weight), blame.
Wyte, to blame; to reproach.

Y
Yard, a garden; a stackyard.
Yaud, an old mare.
Yealings, coevals.
Yell, dry (milkless).
Yerd, earth.
Yerkit, jerked.
Yerl, earl.
Ye'se, ye shall.
Yestreen, last night.
Yett, a gate.
Yeuk, to itch.
Yill, ale.
Yill-Caup, ale-stoup.
Yird, yearth, earth.

Yokin, yoking; a spell;
    a day's work.
Yon, yonder.
'Yont, beyond.

Yowe, ewe.
Yowie, dim. of ewe; a pet ewe.
Yule, Christmas.